BLUEPRINT PROMISE

BLUEPRINT PROMISE

*How To Build Blueprints that
reflect your subconscious thinking*

ORVILLE GILMORE JR.

BLUEPRINT PROMISE
HOW TO BUILD BLUEPRINTS THAT REFLECT
YOUR SUBCONSCIOUS THINKING

iUniverse books may be ordered through booksellers or by contacting:

iUniverse
1663 Liberty Drive
Bloomington, IN 47403
www.iuniverse.com
1-800-Authors (1-800-288-4677)

Because of the dynamic nature of the Internet, any web addresses or links contained in this book may have changed since publication and may no longer be valid. The views expressed in this work are solely those of the author and do not necessarily reflect the views of the publisher, and the publisher hereby disclaims any responsibility for them.

Any people depicted in stock imagery provided by Thinkstock are models, and such images are being used for illustrative purposes only. Certain stock imagery © Thinkstock.

ISBN: 978-1-4917-4959-3 (sc)
ISBN: 978-1-4917-4960-9 (e)

Library of Congress Control Number: 2014918205

Printed in the United States of America.

iUniverse rev. date: 10/14/2014

To My Mother
Thanks for all the Extra Love.

CONTENTS

INTRODUCTION

If you have a vision of a particular lifestyle, *and no map* to get there, this book is for you. It represents a change in thinking with a fifth dimensional mindset. The fifth dimensional mindset is an awareness of the access you have beyond intelligence. Therefore, you can operate with spiritual discernment. As done before the bite of the Apple.

It illustrates a belief supported by the word that says through discerning wisdom, knowledge and understanding come. It is a belief that says *through prayer all needs are met.* Many of us have found that the work we put in does not come close to the rewards we received. This book takes a close at why.

Thomas Paine one of the founding fathers who's philosophy influenced the philosophy reflected in the Declaration of Independence said, *"These are the times that try men's souls"*, and the Rev. Martin Luther King Jr. who's thought-provoking speeches stirred the nation said," Change does not roll in on the wheels of inevitability, but comes through continuous struggle."

Indeed, the problem is not the people. Trying to live democratically in a world where the kingdom lifestyle, demands a relationship with the sovereign government of God, represents a major problem.

As a result, *most of us find ourselves lacking knowledge beyond human comprehension* and left with the natural man's mentality to solve problems.

In my previous, book "Who You Gonna Blame It On?" We discussed techniques to recognize your-life by working with a journal. One must know thyself in order to recognize areas that must change, to sustain the lifestyle you seek. *Seeing stages of your life on paper presents a manageable way to change.*

This book "Blueprint Promise" is intended for reading by all people. *It is a continuing glimpse* into the building blocks of the roadmap *needed to reach that desired lifestyle.*

The words expressed within this book are basic to the ideas and insights developed by the lines of communication provided by my maker with the express purpose of serving all situations, and are used to **present a lifestyle of success surrounded with peace of mind.**

The mouthpiece for producing and sharing these ideas and insights, *Orville Gilmore, from the west side of Chicago has himself become one of the success stories brought about from such lines of communication.* The company he keeps is committed to the explosion of light wherever anyone is willing to listen.

"Blueprint Promise" is a formula for transforming people and their thoughts from the vales of intellect to the peaks of discernment. It drips of inspiration, revels in the exploits of faith, and identifies guidelines for those in search of a knowing lifestyle.

Good people often find themselves envious of those who use corruption and the sense of superiority that come with it. They also seem to have no problem money can't solve. They don't toil in two jobs to make ends meet.

For me personally the worst comes in the form of verbal attacks they spew about the word of God. They will ask, where is my reward, for having faith in the spiritual realm.

Here's what **I believe**, the spiritual realm is invisible but manifest itself in the physical realm. To reach into this invisible realm you have to weaken your flesh, by doing this the word becomes louder and discernment of it becomes clear with directions. Practicing this message will build faith. *Spirit-to-spirit teaching it's called, will shine light on your destiny,* and prepare you for that journey.

Most of us are moving at such a pace that we find ourselves feeding the problem. We must grow with the problem, ***which is the never-ending growth of weeds*** that pop up at every turn in our lives, and with the added feature of the media playing to our flesh, we can no longer use intellectual arguments to kill the weeds, **we must spray them with spiritual teachings**.

- Why do approximately 80% of the people never realize their goals?
- Why do we fear failure?
- Why does analysis breed paralysis
- What lessons are we not learning?
- With all the information available, why are so few successful.

This book has timeless solutions to these questions and more.

ACKNOWLEDGMENTS

I would like to thank the many people who patiently listened to the ideas that are presented in this book as well as the support needed at critical times to complete it.

To the family, we are a blessed people.

To the Woman in my life, whose dedication to the truth and love for me, in both business and in the ideas we shared together. Thank you for loving me the way you do.

To Megan and Quincy, who has given me many rewards that only a father can understand. Keep up the good work, and thank you. To Ericka, you are from royalty, represent!

To Dwayne, who has always had my back I love you brother.

To my sisters Sheree and Loren whose talent is undeniable and unmatched thank you for sharing your skills.

To my boys in the Minne-apple, Chicago, Detroit, Seattle and Las Vegas as well my brother Dwayne thank you for the commitment to the truth as you see it, as well as the balance you brought to the table when there seemed to be no reason to do so, thank you.

To all my readers who continue to support my work and have put trust in my integrity you have my appreciation. Thank you.

To my mother who laid a foundation of persistence, and a true trailblazer thank you.

Orville Gilmore Jr.

To my stepfathers, Larry and Forest whose wisdom always proved correct, thank you for being real Men.

Finally, to my Lord and Savior Jesus Christ, thank you for blessing this work.

Chapter 1

PREPARE TO TAKE ACTION

There are two concepts, which, if you understand and take to the meditation level you will create a breathtaking and gratifying lifestyle for you and your family. Ignore them, and you will likely find yourself in the *"Twilight Zone"* where chaos rules.

The first concept involves *the characteristics of preparation.* Look at your favorite champion, or a famous character; they all have one thing in common the seeds of preparation. Colin Powell the 65th US Secretary of State when asked about career advice said, "There are no secrets to success. It is the result of preparation hard work and learning from failure." Confucius was a Chinese social philosopher who deeply influenced East Asian lifestyles said success depends on previous preparation, and without such preparation, there is sure to be failure. In the sports arena I would say there is nothing like training and preparation. Venus Williams, tennis champion. When asked, how to you do it said you have to train your mind as well as your body.

Look at the list below. Understanding and applying these characteristics will create and develop the mindset of a champion of any lifestyle you desire.

- Defining the nature of the playing field
- Handling and growing with the weeds in the field.
- Focusing on the big picture
- The value of words
- Practice, practice, practice

The second concept, links to preparation, linked to a *spiritual base together you can now develop a blueprint that holds a promise*, not only will it change the way you think, but how you act. When you become committed to this process change is a smooth transition, and can turn any life into an incredibly effective lifestyle. My experience has shown me being prepared has many advantages in crunch time.

Spiritually based action plans will reflect your subconscious thinking, spirit-to-spirit style. Here are seven action steps. Link as many as you can.

- Decide what you want
- Visualize it
- Ask God for it
- Belief you have it
- Thank God for it
- Put it on paper
- Meditate on it

Ignoring the sovereignty of God's government is most unfortunate. Those who do, will rely on something resembling luck, experience constant stagnation, and ultimately stop trying. Settling for whatever comes next. These consequences are relentless without the wisdom of God. You must work the system taught by Jesus your Lord and Savior. He's given us grace so do your part.

This book, then, is about producing results that says you are nothing more than a reflection of your spirit, and subconscious mind, renewed.

If you are unwilling to change, your life will never be capable of giving you the lifestyle you want.

The first change that needs to take place must deal with your vision of a perfect day, from the time you get up in the morning until the time you lay down for the night. What does that life look like? You must be able to express in detail what it looks like to anyone who asks.

The effects of thinking this way help prepare you for the obstacles on the playing field. ***When the playing field is defined, the obstacles will become clear.*** The solutions to these obstacles will depend on your level of discernment of the word, which has authority and will not return void.

The more proficient we become in exercising the authority of God's words, the closer we come to that dreamed lifestyle. This book through the grace of God will help you in that effort.

My prayer is; by the time, you are through reading the book *you will have a better understanding of how the kingdom works* in your life.

Chapter 2

THE PLAYING FIELD

The playing field has many names, athletes call it the arena, those with jobs call it the workplace, CEOs call it the boardroom, if you are in college you might call it the campus, many of the basic lessons for me came from a place called the hood.

Now that I have changed the way I think, *I call it the bible*. Whatever it's called these days there is a belief that this playing field is not level. I agree strongly, *but there are advantages with-in it* and belief is the most promising advantage. There are many more, this book will bring these advantages to your attention.

Let's take a closer look at the field in general. This field is where the game of life is played-out. This field is made of life changing obstacles and redeemable riches.

The obstacles range from problems with our health to lost opportunities. *The biggest obstacles come in the form of addictions. The main addiction is trying to solve problems under the influence of our own understanding.*

We will confront these additions with solutions throughout this book.

This field also contains benefits of redeemable riches such as reduced symptoms of depression and anxiety, a larger sense of awareness and confidence. To name a few, *but the greatest benefit and advantage lies in the fact that you can speak to any situation and expect a change*, teaching how is one of our goals. Planting the seeds of speech is a major part of the preparation. The change in speech is the catalyst for the coming blueprint to become a promise.

There is only one requirement in the field of play and that comes under the heading of flexibility.

Although there is a time for firmness, it's also important to remember how wheat grows with the weeds. The weeds of life are a certainty, and the *discernment of words and it's use as a pesticide will clarify when to bend.* Used properly you become wiser and flexible using better solutions to overcome the obstacles of the playing field.

Discerning how to see things as someone else might see them will also allow you develop solutions, and a better understanding of grace. Grace is a by-product of understanding. *Without knowledge of grace, one becomes inflexible and snap* as soon as the winds of interruptions become stiffer.

The obstacles we like to call problems come with all fields of life. I call them weeds. They seem to grow and grow. *The good news about weeds is they cannot stop the harvest of your life*, and neither can man's solutions. Amen, for that.

Chapter 3

POSSESSING THE PLAYING FIELD

The game begins with the question. How do you grow the lifestyle you desire when the weeds come from the same hole as the seeds?

There are two schools of thought about how to play the game under these circumstances. Many suggest the democratic way, which relies on *your own intellect to solve the problem. The other* side relies on *a spiritual way* to solve the problems. You will find keeping the base solutions at two serves you well.

We will discuss these two ways from another perspective in the next chapter. Going forward it is important to remember, when working *in any field, like farmers we reap the fruits of what we have sown, ten-fold.* This fact is not debatable

Let's look at expanding your perception of the playing field from a spiritual point of view.

From this view, *what you see with your eyes are not the real obstacles*, but you can see them clearly for what they are by using the right combination of words. For example, you say words that reflect grace, be quiet and listen the response to those words will come from the heart backed-up by their history of action. The obstacles are still there. The size of it hasn't changed; all that is needed now is remembering palms 119:105. *The light from the word changes your perception, as a result, you see differently* and because of that, the threat of obstacles will diminish, and the game turns in your favor.

6

The weeds of life we call problems have a job to do. You must look at them as you would a hater. A hater will expose your flaws, and try to knock you down mentally. If they knock you down physically, you have to get up period. With the right pesticide, *(pesticide being your combination of words) these words will bend you in another direction*. Don't think you're going to rid yourself of them. The weeds of life are an inevitable thorn in every person's side. *Just like a rose, you will flourish among the thorns.*

Always *remember the word of God does not come back to him void*. For me, this master key unlocks all things.

Once the problems show themselves, you simply spray them with the word. They will do their job. If you deal with problems properly, they will strengthen your faith. If you don't they will weaken it. The key is a viewpoint of change.

Let's look at the weed from another angle. The weeds persistence can be a stabilizing force in strengthening your faith. *All of us have had a noxious weed attack*. This kind of weed has a tendency to invade all parts of our life, it has a high reproductive growth rate and deep roots complete with its own nutrient system. They are the sharks of the system.

For example, lust is at the top of this list. It has the potential to influence all parts of our life. Like TV, i.e. media, the more you are involved the more it programs the roots of division, and it feeds fear. This threatens our entire way of life.

For most, the knowledge needed to deal with problems is coming from the wrong place. This is where learning from your own understanding can hurt you. *We like to throw money at them*, ignore them, hope they go away, do what you did before, or blame it on someone other than ourselves.

Whatever you choose you are going to have to rely on faith. That being the case, *I suggest you step back and look at it with a broader perspective.*

The best way to do this is by looking at it through the spiritual lens of opportunity. What I mean by that is spirituality will always give you a way out. This solution represents a direction. Believing this is possible, enables you to *look at the totality of what the problem represents.*

Chapter 4

SEED WORK

When you plant a flower in the garden, as soon as it starts to show, parts of a weed appears, you don't pull the weed out because you might also pull the flower out. One waits until the flower is fully grown, then you pull the weed. If you **notice the weed didn't die and neither the flower**. They grew with each other. As it is with life, we must grow with the problems. This perspective is a spiritual one. The flowers purpose is to grow and flourish, it does not worry about the weed. It looks for opportunities to grow. Another entity fights the weed battle. Doors of opportunity open when you looked at it this way.

On the other hand, when you think you have eliminated the problem another one pops up. Like we used to say in the hood G's don't die they just multiply. Think about it for a minute. The Democratic way is limited to man's knowledge and based on intelligence.

What is their philosophy you ask; briefly, it's the belief that the majority of people are always correct.

When I started writing my first book, I spent a lot of time on meditation. *Although I spent 10 years preparing, I had a problem with the many components of publishing*. I heard you needed an editor, a marketer, who would publish it, who would own the rights, how much would it cost, and do I need an agent for starters. It was as if a mountain of details were standing in my way. A friend said to me, stop worrying, the devil is in the details. What I came to understand later was. Like the flower my purpose was to flourish with my surroundings, not linger in the details of how.

In addition, the state of personal affairs looked messy. I was moving to Vegas in a few months, and had not secured a residence yet. My relationship with my son needed consideration, and money was very short. I didn't even have a car. *I just kept writing.*

The one thing I heard constantly was; everyone wants to write a book but very few do. The biggest obstacle came in the form of a sentence. It went like this; *you have been talking about writing a book for almost 10 years and you haven't yet. Just do it, shut up talking about it.*

I just kept writing.

If that wasn't enough my marriage was on the rocks and might be over soon. I had said previously when I retired I was going to write a book, sit on the porch and throw rocks. It now looked further away than ever. *What could I do? It did not look good. The weeds of life looked like they were taking over. I just kept writing.*

As I write these lines, I can recall the taste and flavor of the pity parties.

I didn't really get mad but I did start questioning God, why can't I reach my goals, what does it all mean, what am I missing, I have these urges that I can't seem to do anything about. I am four years into retirement and have nothing to show for it.

My vision was clear the seeds planted 10 years earlier were sprouting new action and faith kept the weeds at bay, and the vision of a book became a reality.

Looking back the keywords I repeatedly used was, "You said" repeating what God had said about promises.

During my first two years of retirement, I lived off my savings. I couldn't work because of my legs, and the cost of living took my entire saving. The pity party was on, and the only guest invited was Mr. Who you gonna blame it on.

That party lasted for about two days. During that time I prayed, I asked God what was next for me I heard nothing. A couple of weeks went by, and I just happened to be watching TV and a preacher talked about not praying the problem, but pray for answers. God will answer and you will get what you need.

Made sense to me so I did just that it felt good and it seemed as if a great weight lifted off my back. In addition, *I started having visions of how I got where I was.* What I had been through and how all my real needs were met.

I never had the riches that you can see (*except for that BMW I use to drive*) but I always had whatever I needed and was happy. *It made me very thankful.* It also let me know, God, was with me and just be patient.

I remember always asking to prepare me for the abundance, because he said test my word to see if it is true.

The time came to make the trip to Vegas and look for a place to live. I had started a journal, which documented the places we thought about, what the crime rate was in those areas, the bus lines and shopping areas, you know things of that nature.

When we got there the second place we looked at hit the target, it had everything, I mean everything we were looking for, two rooms, and two baths, first floor, washer and dryer, pool side in a gated community. Here's the kicker the rent for the efficiency I had in Minneapolis was more than the rent I would pay in Las Vegas. I would save money. You know *I could not say thank you Jesus enough.*

I had been holding the first draft of the manuscript for the book "Who You Gonna Blame It on?" The plan was to self publish, but I had to purchase an ISBN number if I was going to hold all the rights. (*One ISBN number cost over $100*) the ISBN is how you find the book on the market, and the badge of publishers.

I started looking online for a publisher, there had to be a measured way to publish myself. In the meantime, my marriage disintegrated to separation, it was not pretty but I found the answer in the Scriptures. *Matthew 22:23-30 and Luke 18:29 and 30.*

I prayed things go well for her. Only God can judge me. For me this is an example of bending. I felt wiser not to take the advice the world, especially in matters of the heart. Looking at this from a spiritual point of view, opened the door for other possibility, and little did I know what first look like a disaster opened the door for my son to enter.

To have my only son under my wing before he enters the world is a true blessing. God is good. My son now lives with me, and my wife has returned, together we have broken new ground on a notable foundation.

Meanwhile I found a publisher that would do everything I need for a cost I could afford, and just to show you how things work if you believe, the publisher offered me a two book deal for the price of one my cost was less $900.00.

Oh, by the way because my status is disabled I ride public transportation for free, there is a specialized bus that will pick me up and take me anywhere I need to go and bring me back. It also came with a bonus, my son is able to ride with me, to see and discern how to operate in public.

Looking back through a spiritual lens, there had always been a proven formula to deal with weeds. It was in place from the foundation of the world. *Fear almost turned me around, I had to minimize that noise so discernment could speak.*

My desire to retire at age 55 arrived and I took it. I also had a new direction, leading to building a retirement lifestyle. *It turns out I was preparing for a retirement before I knew I was.*

This was for me reaching into the invisible realm and receiving the gift as I spoke about 10 years eairler.

Although I retired under the flag of disability this so-called problem represented a door into the lifestyle I always dreamed about. As I speak to this so-called disability this too shall pass so here I am living the dream.

One of the great lessons is the fact that the devil is in the details. Details turned out to be my intelligence playing chess with the game of life.

Therefore, when new problems arrive, or should I say weeds in your life. Having kingdom perspectives will give you a way out as promised by the King. When looking at the playing field with a spiritual perspective. The wisdom of discernment comes and changes everything.

Decide what you want, visualize it, be patient listen to God, except the fact that his plan is perfect and believe that every step you take is in that plan was predicted according to the will of your God. His blueprint is the promise.

These first two chapters speak to preparing for the field before the action. Don't be fooled. Many great men and women have been broken down in preparation for the work they must do in the field. One of my goals is to serve as a signpost in the field of play. Some know me as the right corner. Staying with this message, next we look at preparation and the big picture.

Chapter 5

THE BIG PICTURE PERSPECTIVE

People are fed-up with the current templates of examples that use manipulation of laws to promote fear in order to govern behavior. Looking at this with a big picture perspective, utilizes a higher reality reachable by everyone. The pathway to this higher reality is not based on intellects or reasoning but faith. Faith in the words you use.

This higher reality is a spiritual law, one that works. To tap into this law of faith you must acknowledge that it exists. For example, many will close a prayer by saying, "In Jesus name." Why, Jesus said, whatever you ask in my name I will do. Have faith, in John chapter 14 versus 12-14.

Life is a series of events, and until we have reached the end of the series, it's hard to understand exactly why things happen the way they do. That's one reason to give respect to the elderly. Through the course of life experience, they have seen the puzzle pieces fall into place more times than not.

What we have here is a failure to communicate. The truth is we are here on the playing field for a short time. We do not often see the "Big Picture." You can spend a lifetime trying to figure out what happened before we were here, and what will happen after we're gone. It takes faith to single out one event as a statement of fact.

One of the facts when looking at the big picture is it enhances the many options of the natural world, and its sheer size welcomes fear. Therefore, we must have a new understanding of big picture perspective as it pertains to the lifestyle you desire.

Orville Gilmore Jr.

For me again I try to keep it simple. My understanding of the big picture is enlightened with these essentials.

- there is a line
- there are results that live on each side of the line
- the study of each side reveals one will prove the other
- don't cry about your consequences if you refuse to meditate about both sides
- make a decision

Practically everyone of adult age has heard of stepping over the line. From law-abiding citizen to lawbreaker, from life to death, but the most predominant of all line crossing is moving from darkness into light.

Unsurprisingly the other side of the line is the opposite from which you came. The result will be devastating if you don't understand this, and if you're scared, say you scared. This is the first step, the second step is asking for help. It's very important you think about that last sentence.

Where should the help come from? If you ask the world, you will get a worldly answer. Listen to how that sounds and make you feel. The worldly answers always come with a caveat. A father, freely give help to his children?

Crossing the line without any study of the other side is not wise. That being said, I have found in my study. In order to prove what side is right and worthy I need the other side to prove my point. The philosophy of the other side is the mindset of a weed. We said earlier and further in this book that we must grow with the weeds of life.

If you find yourself on the other side for whatever reason, crying will help you feel good, but you still have to deal with the consequences. You are back to needing help, who do you call?

Study both sides, and make a decision.

Chapter 6

IF YOU'RE SCARED SAY YOU'RE SCARED

Any time a decision offers up change from the norm, it can become a scary proposition. Walking in fear is nerve wrecking by itself. You do not want to make a decision under those circumstances. Because we have to live with this unpleasant atmosphere, it is a necessary to understand its confinement and more importantly its root.

The root of the fear is lack of knowledge. There is nothing more to it. Truth told, any time you understand something confidence follows, along with confidence comes a stronger faith. Let me put it to you this way, you will become scared many times in this life, until understanding comes. You will need help many times. Not to acknowledge this is the root of irrational decisions.

What does the Constitution of heaven we call the Bible say about it, for one fear is confined darkness.

I'm sure you have heard of this saying, "There is nothing new under the sun." The Constitution of heaven can, and will prove that. Don't believe me read for yourself. If you're scared of what the bible will do to or for you say, you're scared. You're going to like the words of the Constitution, It will take away the fear and makes you look good, I guarantee it.

The bible is the true path of enlightenment. The information presented in this book will take you to its doorstep.

In order to arrive at the lifestyle you deserve it is vital to understand where you are in the big picture. Put these answers on paper, what happens next will amaze you.

- Where are you're trying to go to
- Why do you need to get there

- What's the best route
- What will I need
- Who is going with me
- What price will I have to pay

Meditate on these answers, and experience spiritual law of faith at work.

Chapter 7

SOW WHAT

If you are not satisfied with the yield that has been produced from your actions, you now must sow new seeds. Forget about the past. Just do it. It's that simple.

A seed, when placed in the ground, is under the surface in a dark, cold and muddy place. The seed then begins to germinate. To the onlooker, it looks like its demise. Then, at the very moment that the seed has completely broken down, something extraordinary happens. It begins to sprout. When it breaks through the surface all we'll see is the beauty of it. The word will work in your life just like that seed.

Think about your life, your career, relationships with others and with God. When your speech became negative, results got negative. That is when others, and circumstances set the agendas for our lives. Looking at this from a big picture perspective gives you different answers and a new direction.

These next few pages and chapters are intended to give you a different perspective of the big picture with life changing techniques. These are not new, just another view.

What does life look like for you? **STOP HERE**; think about it for a minute. Write it down in your journal, if you do not have one now is the time.

What would your life look like captured on film, would you (or anyone else) want to watch it? By taking a mental step back, the view will always show you the change needed for your next move. **Repeat this exercise often**.

To most, life is all about perception. What one person sees as reality is completely different from what another person in the same situation sees. It all depends on how you think, and feel about it, and the behaviors it prompts. Trying to satisfy others and make no waves ushers in a picture that will shape your world to someone else's perception.

In a busy life, it can be tough to find the time and space to take a step back and look at the bigger picture. The why question, must be followed by silence. Silence is a seed that will quiet the noise of the senses, making room for the chain reaction of new thoughts.

For me personally after using this technique the question for me was, if what's needed is given freely what is want. The question of need or want is worthy of another book, but for now it is just food for thought

By taking a step back, and looking at how you reacted to situations, and interacted with other people on paper is one of the most powerful techniques on earth, we would learn considerably more about ourselves. It is in this self-awareness that we ultimately find order, and plant new seeds.

In the formulation of your thoughts, you must be truthful. If you live beyond your means, you will always come up short. If you don't have a budget, you will not know where your money is going. If you are not prepared, you will not be ready.

If the *first* thing that comes out of your mouth are lies, the results will never be right. We all have lied. The seed of a lie blossoms into multiple lies. Once again, we must look at the root of lies, for change, and understand who is the father of lies.

After crossing, the line from truth to a lie in my own life in the short term was all good, but in the end, it nearly cost me everything. There is no light in a lie. Concealed is everything. A lie cannot become the truth, no matter how you twist it.

For those who must see, to believe, a journal of just the results of your decisions can become your first book. How can you straighten out something you know nothing about? As the man said, you don't know me you just think you know me.

I'm not talking about the outside of you I'm talking about the inside of you because what's inside will come out, and if you don't know what's coming out there will be no order, your status is inflated, and you will be in the twilight zone, a place that will keep you in fear of the future.

When this truth is on paper, you have the opportunity to break it down into smaller manageable pieces. Your next step is to look at the source of each piece. Knowing the source, allows you to interact with it in ways that show on the outside.

Chapter 8

TRUST AND ACCEPTANCE

Everyone has defects, and flaws. They feed on disorder and disbelief. When they appear, we call them weakness and the mistakes of a person. Look long enough and you will see them. Look at yourself long enough you will see them again.

It's easy to accept this fact in others, but almost impossible for ourselves. This is the first level of truth. Acceptance will be painful. The blame game is the only alternative.

Because these facts are initially hidden and carefully camouflaged, trust has to be established. The art of accepting people's defects and flaws favorably depends on the confidence you have in your God, or man's solutions of acceptance.

Both types of transparencies promote trust and acceptance, but only one comes with the guarantee of grace. The only thing left is to choose which side of the line, or system you will work. Those grasshoppers who jump from one side to the other side will never settle down. Joy will be short-lived because you have to jump again.

There is a line in the sand. I call it a lifeline. Intelligence tells us each side has the wherewithal and the resources to dominate its own side, and they seem to be at equal strengths. You made a decision to put in work on one side or the other, now you must trust and accept, with the expectations of deliverance, trusting you have made the right choice.

Your study of the source (*The Maker*) of each side will identify which route to choose, alone with their governing rules of enlightenment, your readiness for what happens next in part is a characteristic of this book.

Right now, I like to stop here and make this point.

Before learning anything or preparing for something, before we gain knowledge we are in the dark. If you think, you have learned, prepared, and discerned enough to gain the correct knowledge, but continue to fail, stop fooling yourself. You are still in the dark. We are not trilobites.

Another point I like to make stands in the fact that one of these systems do not base its success on the democratic ways of life. This alone is a problem for most.

What kind of seed did you plant? Seeds of the word brought to you by Jesus, during their germination stage set-up lines of communication, and broke down your situation only to light up a new path. If you ignored it or missed it the first time, never fear it's a continuous loop in your subconscious mind. All that is required to activate is silence.

When this inside action breaks the surface, like any flower the light of the *Son* pulls you closer to him. I personally trust and accept this sentence.

My mother still says act as if you have it until you do. It's the same as walk by faith not by sight. Is this not the same thing? In addition, in America, getting is not the problem, how you get it, is. Believing what you can't see is a relatively easy thing to do, and one of the seeds of solving any problem. Once you know how.

All techniques of preparation used in this book starts with looking at your vision in a spiritual way with the understanding it's the future of success. Looking at it from a human perspective will give you a human's best answer, which is flawed. What man is perfect? Knowing this makes it acceptable to look for outside help. With that help, you can start to chart your way to a better future.

Attaching words to your vision will act as glue and in effect call for the action needed for success. ***In the next chapter, I will deal with the value of these words.***

You cannot get rid of the insolence of people. When it comes to interacting with others, especially for those of you who know you do not play well with others. Silence will open up new lines of communication that work for you. The system today is using its entire means to rid itself of its own harvest of influenced insolence. Opposing any analysis, and peddling the idea that we must live and grow with their schemes of greed. This just begs the question. Whom do you trust? Furthermore, whose job is it to pull these weeds from our lives?

There is no getting around it, one must prepare itself for the coming onslaught and practices of the media, the universities and the financial systems that back this noise machine.

Our goal is to prepare you to comprehend the effects of this noise at its entrance points. Doing so will alter the decision process. Keeping this noise at a low volume, gives the voice of enlightenment a chance. Clarity is necessary, if you want change in your life.

My definition of success changes depending on the situation, change that brings order and balance is always the goal. The key is to slow everything down. This allows you to break everything down. Order always follows Chaos. What we tried to illuminate in this book is to hold that order until the next decision.

This world started with order, then fail into chaos. Now, here comes order. Could it be the circle of life?

We all need help in the way we handle the noise machine. The DNA of help consist of

- making a decision
- believe that decision will happen
- act as if you already have it
- give praise to your God

If asking for help is a distorted principle, the treadmill awaits and all you need now is a gerbil uniform. If not, it is wise in my opinion to get a working understanding of the DNA of help.

Get over yourself and ask the source for help. The source is your Lord and Savior Jesus Christ. The wisest among us search for his teachings.

From my personal experience, his words are spiritual in nature, seeded in visualization and watered with faith. Most believe there is evil, and good is the answer to it, or vice versa. After trying both sides, it's clear that one road is narrow and the other wide. Another distinction lives in the fact that light is needed on the narrow road, and attainment from personal to physical pulls you down the wide road. The one difference I found most intriguing was, one road leads to a sovereign government the other leads to a subjective government.

It would be wise to examine these distinctions for yourself.

Chapter 9

VALUE OF WORDS PART 1

From the OG to the hip-hop nation

Welcome to kleptocracy, and his good friend democracy. I call this game insanity. Play it to long you become an atrocity. This will affect your cardiology. Now you live a life of despondency riding the roads of redundancy, conspiracy, jealousy and buffoonery.

We seemed lost in foreign policies, and rotten ideologies, have we become a mockery. We come from the royal authority that rules by the hand of sovereignty. Getting back in harmony will require a bit of urgency. Slow down look around ease up on the ferocity, and take a long at your philosophy.

Before your style becomes an elixir and part of this world as a fixture, I suggest you take part in the big picture.

Look at the curses that make life a circus. It's your versus that laced the surface of screwed up circuits. In order to fix this you need a new list of words that don't twist and dismiss the wisdom of the kingdom in this public address system. With a straight face, lace the texture with love, about the big picture.

Look at decisions that affect your visions are they emissions that lead to imprison or are they ammunition that starts a petition that has no precision and yet you believe in your rhetorician. This to my friend is a natural mixture added to the look of the big picture.

It's high treason to not know the reason you exist in this region. Knowing the season will give you cohesion, it doesn't matter that the field is uneven. A plan is necessary for the blueprint to become formulary, and visionary. Then your efforts will become legendary.

It's not easy to capture your life in one chapter. In order to fracture the ultimate hacker and regain that swagger, you must deal with the King and his subject matter.

Adding the right ampullar can make your life spectacular but you can't pick-her, that is the kicker, life can be richer if this is adding to the big picture.

Gravitational interaction is a reaction to the action. I'm breaking it down to a coming attraction, living in accord and satisfaction. When the skin leads the way it's a conversion reaction that leads with passion, now this chemical reaction spells dissatisfaction with a capital distraction.

Now you are missing in action for a bit of that smash'in. Listen up young bloods to this miniature description set in the world of encryption. Listen to the fixer as he drawls the big picture.

The way you think is the missing link, and if you don't use ink, your game will be rinky-dink, your mentals will stink, you've got to watch what you drink it could lead to the sink now your life is a wink because all you have left is the lip-sync.

To realize your dream you must not use the green on and immorality scheme, just pray the unseen. Lean on the lessons of the smoke screen. It's obscene to address the machine without the knowledge of the King, if you know what I mean. If your game has no scriptures you will end up a trickster I suggest you add a few it to the mixture, just ask any victor, it's always in their big picture.

Now that you recognize that game and the prize, stop with the lies pray to be wise pullback the disguise from the works of devise. Forget the list price and take the advice from the one who comes twice.

Stop rolling the dice, no need for all that ice just keep your father in the line of sight. All you need is a slice of his might. So take my advice when your game takes flight from that inner site let there be light for you only live twice.

What does all of this mean in the big scheme of things? If you look to the sky for the most high, you'll stop the demise, and be baptized with all the supplies you need to arrive. This implies you don't need the lies, and won't have to disguise all your enterprise then lose it all for a shady compromise it might be wise to forget the tough guys. You will have to mature in order to procure, take a look my friend at the big picture for sure.

These illustrations are visions of preparation to start the foundation that prepares us for revelation to start the elevation of self-perpetuation. This is not the time for hesitation, let go of the world organization there is no future in retaliation. Invest in vertical integration with the holy congregation and feast of the dedication become part of the proliferation of the instrumentation from the King of creation.

Conclusion:

Did you notice how some words created pictures, and stories. Creating a vision behind your own words is a powerful tool to use. Practice using this technique will pull you ever closer to the promise of any dream.

Preparation is already a big part of your life. Sit back for a minute and stop reading. Think about how you prepared for this day.

In order for you to receive your future blessings, you must mentally prepare to accept them where you are.

If you already started this process, make the picture clearer by adding color and more action. Pictures make dreams receptive to the possibilities of the life you want, and evidence you need to move forward with this process.

Without preparation, and practice it's Willy-Nelly time

In these next pages, we will talk more about the value of words and the gravitational interaction with the pictures or visions that come with those words.

Chapter 10

VALUE OF WORDS PART 2

Return of the words

So far we have talked about the perspective of the playing field, we also talked about how visions help develop a plan in a big picture way. These words literally carry change, cut like a knife and have the weight of life and death. For example, used properly these words have the power of conversion, and gets straight to the point, they breathes life into your dream. A great illustration of this comes in the form of the reaction to music.

Using key words to describe your vision is a technique used, and practiced by those who stay on course. One must measure the words that come out of one's mouth.

We said in regards to the playing field; the words we use would have the power to diminish the threat of influence that would otherwise take you off course. Case in point, remember the last time something was said or done to you that made your blood boil, everything changed, first your face, then your words and last but not least your attitude. You were completely out of focus. Remember that moment. Most dangerously, those words introduced a worldly point of view.

Let me give you a page out of my own life in this regard.

In the workplace, I used my mouth as a shield and if you were an irritant and approached, the wrong way or I deemed you an enemy I made sure the words of profanity would show you a side from the depths of hell.

In my mind, fighting hate with hate was the only way to keep the haters off my back, since it looked like it worked, I got better at it but thank God, there were people in my life that reminded me of how this behavior would eventually turn my blessing into plagues.

My answer to those friends was always the same. "I hear you talk 'in, and continued walk 'in." It didn't take long to re-learn the lesson, hate cannot conquer hate. The greatest hater will always win the hate game. It was the power of words personified.

At the time of these rants, the power of my words forced the haters to back away. They clearly were not used in the spirit of God, as I said they were from the depths of hell.

Over time, that inward language became an outward dialogue. My blessing slowly turns into plagues just as my friend Ms. Berry in particular had predicted.

This was the first of many real lessons in the value of words, and one of the greatest lessons discerned to date. The clearest example I can give you at this time is to examine the lifestyle of a person who's every other word is a curse word, and see for yourself the power and results of their words.

I found out the hard way that the return on your words produces a beneficial lifestyle or a contemptuous one. In the end if you don't find a way to control or restrain your words you will find yourself condemned by the action they create, and justify your treatment.

Lesson one; words should always be consistent with the understanding of grace. Grace is a gift from God not the results of your work. It is unmerited favor.

Look at how many times you did wrong in your own life. The number is so high you could not stand before your maker and say you are worthy. Grace allowed you forgiveness, and to stand before your God, yet most cannot forgive, but want forgiveness.

Words should carry out the ***covenant of salt,*** which is both, savory and wholesome. This raises your consciousness to a higher level of understanding. Do yourself a favor and invest in the word "Grace" it is transformational.

One method I used to raise my consciousness to a higher level of understanding came when I read the words written in red in the Bible. At an early age, I was told that the words in red were the words spoken by Jesus and his words would change your life.

I didn't know at the time that God's word is our source of authority, and it will always take away obstacles. I came to understand this as I matured. Now I pass it on to you.

For example, in my football life as a defensive back I used certain words in combination to overpowered 99% of all receivers who came before me, even when practicing. Those words misunderstood brought bitterness; the way it ended made me bitter, thus, my words changed.

When that dream of Pro football was over I prayed and asked why, what did I do wrong and what now? To make a long story short my mistakes were shown to me, what I absolutely did wrong, and what I should do next.

The answers hurt I went to the blame game and into the twilight zone. When I finally accepted what was shown to me, and believed what the future held, my words changed and my future, the one I'm enjoying now.

The words I use in my football life powered the five senses. By asking God for the discernment of my history without fully knowing actually turned down the noise. What I noticed was his word was constant and now much louder.

Chapter 11

VALUE OF WORDS PART 3

When it comes to preparation, your words will promote the action needed to advance your belief system. Your belief in the authority words have depends on your faith in them. To increase your faith you need to use the words of God often. It's like lifting weights the more you lift the stronger you get.

When your belief is strong enough the fruit from the seeds of your speech, which are born in your heart, will outwardly produce a visible lifestyle and embrace the principles of God's kingdom.

This is how you define success!

In the light of the times we live in, it is important for one to understand the authority and power words carry. Understanding will allow you to take from the spiritual realm and manifest itself in the physical.

The fact of the matter is God created things with words, and so can we because we are in his image. When Adam sinned, his spirit lost it communication skills of discernment. Consequently, his words lost the power they had. Jesus got it all back. Can I get an, Amen to that!

Preparation is nothing more than practicing, what do you think practice what you preach means. If you are willing to do this at each level of planning, your words will easily influence your faith, the buildup will expose the roots of fear. Once fear is contaminated, with faith, the blueprint promise will become a reality. This fight has been going on as long as you and I can remember. Today words can still get you killed but used properly you will never die. My weapon of choice, is the word, what about you?

Chapter 12

STRATEGY MINDSET

"We are born supernatural; you are made perfect through the process of diligent practice in the usage of the word." (*Blueprint Master*)

Practice is a pursuit to improve skills, customary behavior, and a method of learning by repetition, rehearsing repeatedly for the purpose of mastery. We all know repetition is the mother of skill. The greatest gift that practice can give is unseen. It is the gift of faith. Practiced will change your behavior and put you on the path of mastering self. It makes perfect sense to practice.

Life seems to offer so many problems the question becomes what should we practice first. Communication skills would be a good place to start, or should I practice moderation with my eating habits, what about money, do I practice generosity or instant gratification.

Here's the kicker I could practice day and night 24, seven 365 and still lose according to the world. I say you never lose just discern, but more valuable than that is what you become because you practiced.

People normally practice long enough to accomplish a particular goal. For instance, you use good relationship techniques until you win their hand. We eat smaller portions until the weight is loss, and finally we save enough money for that down payment.

Warning! If practiced becomes passé after your goal is reached you may be a grasshopper hopping back and forth living in a world of inconsistency wondering why you take two steps forward three steps back.

From the perspective of what you become we all understand one gets better physically. My concern is the mindset. What you can't see is your change in thinking. Practicing is self-replicating it becomes contagious to the rest of your activities. It is the medicine of champions.

One of the techniques talked about in my first book deals with breaking down perceived problems into smaller parts. You are familiar with divide and conquer aren't you.

In regards to fear and thinking, fear should be a recipe for change. However, it can be the biggest deterrent ever. The repercussions for not dealing with either side of fear in your own life will be devastating, and attack when you least expect it.

Can we agree that we all need practice; depending on the problem, we can also agree that for most there is no clear starting point. **I suggest you start with yourself**. You should know the absence of practice is a doorway to irrational decisions. Without practice, fear has a clear path to dominate the senses

We intend to expose and demising the power of fear at its entry point. We know knowledge is the kryptonite to fear. When breaking the body down I noticed fear is magnified through our senses. Therefore, study the effects of fear and your senses. Below are some guidelines for the purpose of focus.

- you cannot blame anyone else you are the starting point.
- what are you designed for and what are you asking
- who and where is your help coming from.

I am the workmanship of my creator. I am a spirit in the shell made of dirt; my design is for the glory of God. I ask for things hoping its in his will for me. If you don't know his will, ask for that. The study of your senses and the effects of fear alone will change the way you look at things.

I will dig deeper into this subject later in this book.

Everyone and everything has a role to play. We must grow with it all.

Strategy is always tied to action and action is always tied to practice, below are some of the strategies meant to attract positive outcomes.

- recognize your design, and follow the laws of it
- work from the accumulated documents that define you known as your journal
- study why you believe what you believe
- find a way to hear and read the word

Okay, you are a spirit; the question now is how one communicates with a spirit. Secondly, how does one practice faith.

Practicing faith is developing a relationship with the spirit of truth, or the Holy Spirit. He comes from the father, and will teach and remind us of everything that Jesus said. If you quiet your senses, you will hear him.

Faith comes by hearing then practicing what you heard. Reading is another form of a relationship.

Squeeze out pride when it comes to communications. Every time you put God first you push pride back one step, keep pushing and it will fall off your life. Now the voice of the helper you will hear.

Practices means confidence, this prepares new revelations for all situations. You have heard it said, my word is my bond. In God's Kingdom he says, I watch over my Word, it will not come back void.

Start by believing God. The more you read the stronger your faith. This will contaminate fear, once the contamination starts it,'s just a matter of time before others see the authority of your words. Glory to God.

You being a spirit must to be taught spiritually a dog cannot teach cats the language of dogs, and if you are not spiritual, you cannot understand spiritual teaching.

Here's a little rhyme just to remind.

This is that one stop shop for the information drop, from that little black book that swings a spiritual hook. Open it up and take a real good look, if it seems odd it's because of your public façade, this is your wake-up call squad, coming from the word of God.

Practice will define the playing field. Give you the perspective of things to come; this big picture view will change your words, alone with your tactics. The only thing left is practice, practice, and practice.

This is my personal big picture mindset that maintains my lifestyle.

- **The goal**...To contaminate fear
- **Strategy**...Reach into the unseen and bring into site
- **Daily plan**...Pray for the vision and empowerment
- **Journaling**...Record for the next generation
- **Live and teach simply**...Rid myself of the unnecessary and unessential things

Chapter 13

OVERVIEW OF PREPARATION

1. Decide what you want
2. Visualize it
3. Ask God for it
4. Believe you have it
5. Thank God for it
6. Put it on paper
7. Meditate on it

There is no dispute, Jesus was here as a prophet to redeem his lost sheep. It's time we believe what he said. There is enough evidence for those who have ears to hear, for those who have faith and for those who believe in everlasting life. Let us not forget those that don't believe, you too will come to understand.

There is written and unseen evidence in the world that the earth is the field we play on and the authority to rule over it. The future in part lies in preparation and your view of the big picture. The values we place on the words we use determine how we live and practice will strengthen our faith.

You have a part to play in this redemption process consequently; one is taught just as a parent teaches a child. Teaching works best in progression just like math. In math you can't get to five before three, you are taught one, two, three, four, and five. Thusly, it is with the King of Kings.

When your parent believed you were ready, they ask you to decide what you want out of life. Did you ever think about the fact that they provided what you needed before you even thought about what you wanted. Most parents teach you to see yourself as they see you and to do what they did.

Many of those same parents will also tell you to ask God for the things you want, just as they did and he will provide you with them. For that reason, your part in this redemption process starts with an understanding that your needs are already met. You just have to decide what you want.

With limited understanding of God and the way of the world, needing proof before movement puts most under time. Thanking God will take more discerning of your life. Meanwhile the seesaw continues and thanking God shrinks until the highest level of danger is imminent.

We've been rescued because of grace, but that too is not understood by most. Forgiving others regularly also shrinks because of this.

To make a long story short the next step comes by way of action either visualized or discerned by way of schooling. Be it at the University level, where words are larger and have multiple meanings, the street system, where the wrong choice of words will get you killed the natural system where loopholes run amok or the supernatural system where one rules and takes care of all needs. Either way you come out of it with a level of knowledge and a vision of yourself, the world and your mission.

Your discernment of whatever way you choose will determine your success on the playing field.

Here's a twist on that process. Let's play a word game.

What image does the word paper conjure up, and what use do you have for it. Most think of money, and spending it. Paper plays a major role in schooling of all kind. The answers are on paper. The way you view it establishes your priorities. Looking at you on paper will unravel this twist.

This very slight adjustment of how you visualize words on paper makes all the difference in the world. Some say do what you love and the paper will follow. I say to discern your design and everlasting life will follow.

For most, this understanding is the first real picture of any lifestyle. Slight adjustments in word use and the practice of it will also expose how you view your strengths and weaknesses.

This is where practice meets preparation. Visualize it first.

Whichever route you decide to go with belief and meditation will elevate Revelation knowledge.

Meditation for our purposes is the practice of focusing your attention, giving you a clear line of communication and awareness of what you must do to take control and maintain that lifestyle you've asked for.

Grasshopper alert! Grasshopper alert!

The demands of the systems of the world will present several ways as the best way throughout your life until you decide on one. This is the grasshopper way. In the end, there is only one way. There is no doubt the more you age the narrower these roads get. ***Warning!*** You need light on whatever road you choose.

The clue is you cannot stand divided you must choose one. Maturity and wisdom will teach you that every creature from the air to the bottom of the Sea has a gift. Man has the greatest gift, grace.

"In one form or another we love, honor, praise, believe, and thank the maker. We admire the work. Ultimately, we ask and pray to the maker. We make the greatest mistake when we worship those gifts instead of the maker of them." (Blueprint Master 2020)

The first part of this book is my effort using my gift from God to prepare and present a way to transform your thinking to realize a desired destiny, on paper.

The second part of this book will deal with the action plan. The blueprint promise is also a map of preparation designed to light you up.

Chapter 14

DEVELOPING A LIFESTYLE MAP

A lifestyle map is like any other map in one regard, it features critical information that leads to a destination. However, it differs from the average map in the sense that its design to inspire, motivate, comfort, instruct and clarify a direction that is spiritual in nature and leads to the gifts laid up for you in the unseen spiritual realm. Your faith in this journey will allow you to pull those gifts down into the physical world.

This is a skeleton of my map.

- The Blueprint Master - the one who spied out the land
- The ingredients - My history, visions, helpers, prayer, obedience, compass, faith, and the word of God that promote action
- Meditating on the destination
- Communicating with the inner man
- My goal- rely on the anchors of the kingdom lifestyle

Arriving at that desired lifestyle is not going to be easy, it's going to take discipline, practice, and faith the size of a mustard seed. The very first thing is to know thy-self. The best way to do this is by journaling. We covered this ground in book one titled, **"Who You Gonna Blame It On"**. You will expose yourself through your own words on paper. This is the power of journaling, and it delivers just enough light to show you a new way.

It is always a wonderful thing when you see without your eyes. In reading my journal, I began to replay the past in my head. These replays clearly exposed mistakes. My journal spied out the obstacles in the land of me.

With obstacles exposed, I would look for other ways I could have done it better. Also during this time, a little voice kept saying ask God, but the volume of intelligents was too loud. I finally noticed every time things got quite that little voice got louder and more consistent.

Later I would understand that little voice was the helper. ***The helper is one of the anchors that steady your foundation.***

Subsequently I asked God, and got much more than asked for. With so much information coming, I had to slow down to receive it. Thinking about it turned into meditating on it. This led to thanking Jesus.

Meditating also led to understanding what kind of love it takes to keep working with someone who takes one-step forward and two steps back.

When you ask for discernment of your journal, or dreams meditation follows. Don't ignore isolation during this time it is the key that opens up the door of discernment. This discovery will uncover the manipulation of the five senses.

The spirit is the true leader. ***Eph 1:17.*** It is your flesh verses your spirit. Your flesh led by the senses lead to the root of all problems.

You will also find you need to increase your faith. Increase means letting Gods word provide. If this is not explored, prepare yourself for endless rounds of disappointment.

When developing a lifestyle map history is, the first element dealt with because the story of your history on paper tells the story of who you are and the reasoning behind what you do. Since we train to believe what we see, seeing on paper is the first wake-up call. This is another way of spying out the landscape, for later needed preparation.

The other major purpose of your history on paper reveals the subtle changes you must make, when moving in a new direction. You will make better moves with history's account.

Another element in the making of any lifestyle map would be the vision of that lifestyle, a clear picture is mandatory. Without a clear picture, you can't be sure and this contaminates your confidence.

If your confidence erodes, you lose faith and once you have no faith you join someone else's program for security and you become a gerbil running around the wheel of life. It's called the twilight zone, the zone is explained in my previous book.

When your vision becomes a clear picture, help fills in the planks. The one man, one-woman show has a perturbing ending at best. Research of the word helper reveals it's really a flash light. Prayer flows after this understanding. I will leave it right there.

The compass is the right-hand of the helper. Look at John 14:26. Hebrew13:6, and Gen 2:18.What can you do without faith?

Action should be a spiritual playground. Asking for help before any movement gives you the opportunity to adjust to the playing field. ***Controlling your words enforces direction.***

To discern the playground, is the goal.

Meditate. Spend some time developing the big picture. Foundation building comes from the inner man. Living under grace is a good thing. Thank you Father. Jesus is the man.

This is my blueprint mindset in summary:

If I can do this, you can do this. We are heirs of the playing field. ***We own it***. With the trail of success blazed for us. Nothing can stop you if you stay on that well lit path. Taking "*I*" out the planning is major because when you can't do it alone. Who do you call on; furthermore why not call on Jesus every time.

We mentioned earlier, a closer look at action reveals our senses are the roots of action in the natural world. Time shows itself as nothing but a thief that steals dreams if not understood.

Your senses can alter your action in a way that has a spinner effect. These are the obstacles on the playing field of life not seen. Don't be fooled into believing the battle ends with the American dream in tow. Yes you must fight but not with others. Once again, it's the inner man versus the outer man. The outer man wants to control your five senses.

A question one should ask is; out of your time how much is devoted to the teachings of the spiritual way. This is one of many reasons, why it is mandatory we look at time differently.

The process of flipping the time script the righteous way is one of the major unseen topics this book points too. Prepare yourself before you go into action is the mantra of success.

Standing for nothing will get you nothing.

Chapter 15

LIGHT PROVOKING ACTION

In the search, for knowledge we all start in darkness, applying any amount of light will bring forth a picture, that picture discerned spiritually will set up a mindset, manifesting into action.

The second half of this book will be concentrating on the effects of a mindset working without the rush of time, and the synchronized action it brings. The mere thought of taking time out of solutions automatically sets-up new thinkings. Meditating on that is a mindset exercise used by visionaries.

Synchronizing this mindset with no consideration of how long leaves more room for preparation. The word impossible diminishes the process. This kind of light provokes a different kind of action.

One of my goals is to facilitate a better understanding of how your senses control your actions, and how the spirit of God talks to your heart. We will also look at why it seems prayers are not answered. We cover styles of practice that will quiet your senses, and turn up the word. We offer examples of the natural and supernatural ways of ushering in new actions. Finally yet most importantly, we will make an attempt in the hope of changing the way you think.

After reading this book, it will be clear that the road of spiritual change is nothing more than slight adjustments that shine more light on spiritual practices. This type of practice is a blueprint filled with promises, designed by the creator of revelations.

Finally this book is a playground of solutions and lessons that lead to action taught by the Redeemer, and our advocate. His gift of grace came with an undeserved peace of mind. Glory to the Alpha, and Omega of life.

Wisdom says you will never stop gathering knowledge. Yet people destroy themselves for the lack of it. Believing your actions will change without examining how the senses control action is a very painful and difficult lifestyle.

Before action begins, a decision is made. A decision made from information, information brought to the table or your brain through our senses, and naturally, you physically move, or speak.

When you know who you are, and what you are you will recognize and understand the playing field on a different level. Subsequently, better decisions apply, to a game plan. All plans lead to a blueprint of the promises you desired.

The belief that all of your battles are already won, will only enhance your preparation, making your action worthy of praise. For many this comes during the second half of their lives. To you and the next generation ask God for spiritual revelation knowledge then stop, and, listen to those revelations coming from your maker.

As I see it, there are two systems, one based on learning, and the other based on discerning. Learning starts in dark territory, where intelligence rule and have you thinking you have all the answers. This way of thinking will have you buying intelligence for the rest of your life. This may explain why little money means little knowledge. Furthermore, you are limited to your own understanding.

I'm not saying learning is a bad thing. What I am saying is discerning comes before learning. It's a slight adjustment with huge implications. Think about it for a minute.

Discerning means understanding. Understanding is enlightenment. Enlightenment is a line of communication to your maker that leads to the discipline of wise behavior.

Understanding first shines light on learning, leading to wisdom and discipline, instead of the world's way, which leans on its own understanding of learning outside of God's system?

To summarize understanding leads to learning that you are under grace, wisdom says forgive my trespasses as I forgive those who trespass against me. This in turn gives me the discipline to act in accordance with the word. For this reason, God prefers mercy.

Discerning is rooted in enlightenment. Trading discerning for learning was a huge mistake. Adam and Eve learned this firsthand. In the beginning, we used discernment for guidance. In order to come out of the darkness of learning we must once again pick up the light to find our way back too discerning.

It is often said it's not what happens when you fall down it's what actions you choose when you get up. I choose the light that provokes actions derived from discernment.

Chapter 16

THINK LIKE THE KING

We begin with talking about the outer-man. That person the public experiences. The one occupied with the status of their five senses. Then there is the inner man centered by spiritual teaching, and directly linked to discernible wisdom visible to the inner eye.

I call this inner man my spirit.

Every person on earth is linked to spiritual teachings that provide discernible wisdom from the father, and we praise him for that. I offer 1st Chronicles 29: 11-13

I would be remiss if I did not mention that everyone on earth has a broken link. Our sin nature causes this link to break and we spend a lifetime repairing it. Picture a man facing a damn 30 feet wide and 30 feet high. A hole pops open and he covers it with one hand, another hole pops open and he covers it with the other hand, another hole pops open you guessed it he covers it with a foot. You get the picture.

This is the problem with a broken link. To stop that water from breaking down that wall, you will need supernatural intervention. To fix that link that connects you to spiritual teaching and discernible wisdom you also will need supernatural intervention.

The outer man is only a reflection of the inter-man. If you have a damaged link because of something that happened in your life, or it has held together by a few strands, the outer man display will have a pulsating effect. Sometimes you will be strong and sometimes you will be weak. Growth tempered by a need to ask the King for solutions will lead you to think like the king.

The outer-man's showing of a natural man is a dying breed.

One thing is for sure, be it in business, athletics, street-life, or wall street you must understand the playing field before preparing for it, or you will be the first to bite the dust. Practice prepares you for the obstacles on the field. This thought process leads to your first draft of a blueprint. Meditating will clarify this mindset and the promise of it.

For those of you who say, what about the unexpected. I say lean on and have faith in your helper. ***That helper is the spirit of truth.*** It is that constant low volume voice, which the senses will always try to drown out.

The wisest among us believe victory lives in the realm of preparation. The greatest teacher once said I go to prepare a place for you. Coupled with how we discern what we hear are among the major ingredients of victory.

Preparation is never fully seen, but realized by all, when the action begins. If you don't believe in faith, reaction stands ready to go.

You do realize reaction is a reverse movement.

Intelligence tells us if the words do not match-up with what you see, you need further proof, so let's touch it, if that doesn't feel right, and what you see doesn't match-up, then logic becomes the criteria.

Logic tells us we have to experience it. All of us have said at one time or another I smell a rat or something along the line of; that left a bad taste in my mouth.

Can you see from this small sample of the information provided by the senses you could wind up running in circles? Seems to me intelligence coupled with your senses is not the best or real answer.

Let me make this point perfectly clear. Without the word of God in any of your pursuits of knowledge will eventually leave you just short of your goal, and lead to the doors of the twilight zone.

Allow me to introduce you to the twilight zone of the flesh.

This is one of the most important pages in this book. When it comes to the fundamental principles of conduct, there is a distinct difference between right and wrong.

No matter how you feel or what you heard about a person judging them is clearly wrong. Freedom of speech is clearly right.

In the twilight zone of the flesh right and wrong are linked coherently, as a result confusion reigns. Out of this confusion comes sexual immorality. Who has not been guilty of sexual immorality? Never fear, It is the practice of it that spells the end.

Your body houses the Holy Spirit because it is a Temple. A Temple should not be defiled. It is an instrument for righteousness. We should all strive to glorify God with our bodies and spirit; after all, they are his. Have you no-regard for someone else's possessions.

The best thing about this zone is there will always be an exit, just reach up and grab the outstretched arm of your maker. Just ask he will always leave you a way out. Word the wise.

Other faults, such as lying are easily conquered, because they work outside of your body. Sexual immorality is different from all other sin because you defile your temple with sexual perversions.

When the intent of lust shows up, we are at the door of the twilight zone of flesh. When you act upon that lust, you have entered.

Action that has confusion written all over it is the biggest clue.

When one of your senses engage, many paths of intelligence are deployed. When used in combinations the word decuple comes to mind, meaning tenfold. The problem I have with intelligence is that it's expensive and come with a sense of entitlement because you paid for it. Intelligence may be inborn but responsibility will be greater. When you think you are entitled, there is a feeling that there is no need to earn anything.

Even at the ground level, it's common to hear, "The game is to be sold not told." This is the natural way of doing things. I call it the way of the gerbil. Where running in circles, is all you do. This is one of the main reasons division is so powerful.

The reason you always run in circles in this scenario is after buying the game it will change, and you must buy and buy again. Exponentially

There is a better way. It is the way of the spirit. In case you did not know you are a spirit, your spirit is inside the shell we call flesh and blood i.e. the body.

The problem is the body responds to the information brought in by your flesh. This information turns into movements. Without control, what kind of life is that?

Your spirit has always talked to you, don't believe me go sit somewhere and be quiet for an hour. The thoughts based in love are the one to live by.

If you can't, it is a clue why thing are not quite right. Your spirit will tell you, clearly, you have to change the way you think. It will be hard to listen because it is different, but fight through it.

Intelligence (*your mind*) will tell you the price of change is too heavy, you have to make many sacrifices. Logically you may think its right but fear of the process tells you, you have run out of time or the time needed for change has run out. Either way you will soon be out. So you settle and whether all storms.

For those who pray, how do you know God hears you, and what did he say. How do you know that voice is his? The answers are in this realm of preparation.

Spiritual teaching is preparation, it tells us to live in the world, but do not be of the world. They say the mind is a terrible thing to waste. I say the mind led by the flesh disguised as intelligence is a terrible thing that guides you.

Here is a quick test of your belief system, is anything in this world freely given? The follow-up question becomes what's the problem. If your answer is yes and no, you are, constantly hopping across the fence, called as needed, ***grasshopper.***

If the answer is no, you need more money. If the answer is yes, keep practicing what is freely given. See 1st Co 2:12

You know intelligents is expensive no matter where you go. The more you have the better you think you can handle any situation. It looks like higher education equates to higher income and riches.

Don't hate if you have little of it. Your path is different and riches will come in another form.

The poor submits quietly to God, and have the most patients. Their answers always have the hint of discernment in them. They always try to be righteous, yet they can barely pay their bills and most live check to check. What are you poor in, what are you rich in.

With all of this on the plate, the poor are happy, and according to Matthew 5:3 theirs is the kingdom of heaven.

The world teaches and preaches you do not have to be poor, the word says the poor will be with us always, go figure. Many believe you can be rich and poor at the same time. I do not.

Take the word poor notice how it changes things. Mainly, the way you feel and think. Think about it long enough confusion may set in. Confusion is a view to many ills. There is no confusion in the word, because of the attachment of discernment.

Therefore, if you fit into the concerns of the poor it is time to reach into the spiritual realm of belief, and pull down your riches into the physical world. If you are rich, it's time to research the mixture of grace and discernment. When you use the words from this mixture, you are also able to reach into that realm and change with the greatest of ease.

This is the level of preparation and action talked about in this book.

Here is an example of the kind of thinking needed to change your life today and tomorrow. Yesterday a man fed over 5000 people with five loaves of bread and 2 fishes. You would have to change the way you think to believe that is possible. What can you think of along this line of thinking?

When visioning about the end game. Working back to front will also change the way you think.

If you start on top without the understanding of grace, your faith is misplaced, and will not save you. It will look like you have no problems, but the fall will be slow and painful.

Chapter 17

BORN TO WIN

If you ask for something and believe, you have received it before you physically get it, is the mind-set needed to win. How you act afterwards defines the level of your belief. Asking is realizing you need help better yet it opens the door of change. Receiving this progression in your heart starts the manifestation process. In this regard, you are reaching into the invisible realm.

After you see this internally, the renewing starts. Your father knows what you need. It's important and a must you ask his will to be your own. The mind is flesh and blood it wants to please you. Quieting down the senses will reveal the truth about what you have seen in your minds' eye.

Practice putting these pictures in writing is the beginning of a lifestyle mapped out, resulting in a blueprint promise.

Be very leery of the words when describing this map to others. They are subconscious keys, that keep you in line with the will of God. Subconscious keys are the thoughts communicated to you when the senses have quieted down.

You will hear me use the word discernment, because we originally communicated with our God this way. If I can get one point across it would be the study of discernment, as taught by Jesus.

The spiritual realm is not seen and the physical world is temporal. They both use the same words with slight variations these variations turn out to be opposites.

In the world of action, you practice your principles that you have deemed the rules of action, if they are wrong you become unclear about the lifestyle you desire. First, you will want this, then you will want that. The key words are *your principle. What are they?*

You are not here to follow your principles of righteousness; you are here to glorify God, alone with his principles.

The principles are basically, his code of conduct and ethics; they must be in line with your vision and you must believe in it. The words you use in this respect will pronounce his vision and rules of action. Remember he enforces his word.

When you know something works you become accessible to it. There is history in the use of the words you choose; it would be wise to study their results. They put thought patterns in motion, which lets you know something about their origin.

The spiritual discernment of grace is a perfect study guide to start this process. For most, this guide will answer most of the why questions, it also appeals to being grateful for what you have now. *There is always someone on the planet who would love to have your lifestyle, no matter what you think of it.*

The world's philosophy

The idea of words creating acts and working closely with preparation is nothing new. You have to look no further than winning programs and the words they use comparably to a losing program and the words they use. Furthermore, these words establish attitudes and provide confidence to act as if you are already on top, or words that keep you frozen in time where losing becomes a practice then a habit.

The world wants you to believe you are a winner or loser before life starts. Their favorite saying is; winners are made not born.

The myth of winning and losing has caused many to start out wrong. You were born a winner. We are all winners according to our design. Examine what it took to get you here.

The history of winners in accordance with this world used the same words when they were losing, they were consistent with those words before they manifested into a winning program. The difference always came in the form of belief.

Let me remind you the world teaches losing is so close to winning a slight edge or a split second will make the difference, and that my friend is the trap door to the twilight zone.

What will you do to gain that split-second or edge?

How many times have people cut in front of you in traffic only to meet them at the next red light.

In a losing program, they say the right words but they don't believe them, and they wonder why the words don't work for them. You will also find there is no faith in losing programs. They learn to accept, then whether the consequences.

Many as a last resort or a life-and-death scenario will ask God for help, he answers with discernment, not intelligence. This is one reason many prayers don't get answered. Discernment always calms you down, gives you new direction, and keeps you from kicking the problem down the road. Either way you have to stop worrying and move on. Has any of this happened to you?

The real World Games

The words of the so-called loser do not put a premium on winning; instead, they promote sportsmanship having fun and exercise. Their make-up are from all lifestyles even the disabled and if they just so happen to win they will celebrate it.

In a so-called winning program, they also promote sportsmanship having fun and exercise. Mindset is the main difference. For example, the people in their program have one look one sound one mindset that starts from the inside smoothly transitioned to an inflated sense of status. Even the disabled in their programs believe their contributions are worthy.

Individuals who display indifference to this concept even in the face of talent eventually are pushed out.

The losing programs mindset is; we win if they screw up, and why have a broken heart trying to win. Everybody is going to play. Let's just have fun and go home.

The so-called losing programs usually have this in common. Approximately 50% of the people in this program believe winning is everything and the other 50% believe the program is just a stepping-stone or a release valve in life's big picture. This programs record will reflect this make-up.

The world would have you believe you must fall under one of these programs. This, my friend is a magic trick. We are all winners.

A closer look will show both scenarios promote controversy and set the stage to distinguish the haves and have-nots. This practice becomes contagious, and puts a premium on economics

My point is the definition of winners and losers is grossly misleading, but their words still carry the weight of empowerment to change things for you or used against you. Many false teachers know this well. Here is the root from which they work; false teachers believe God is the source of evil.

Discernment

Through the eyes of spiritual discernment the so-called loser leans on his/ hers own understanding. The winners lean on discernment, putting all their trust the Lord.

If you put said loser under a macro scope, you will see they win in other arenas maybe arenas that you are looked-upon as a loser. This fact occurs in many organizations as well as the sporting world.

The other fact that exist, in this scenario is, many believe you can be a winner and a loser at the same time. The world says if this is your beliefs, you should work on those things you win at and except the losing as the price of doing business.

This type of thinking attributes to playing both sides of the fence. One side is for the loser, and the other side is for winners. I can see division, can you? In the natural world, they call this one-step forward two-step back.

My personal belief is you either win or discern. Redefine losing replace the word with preparing.

One of the reasons playing both sides of the fence is so appealing is the feature of a short-term fix. The delay seems to give you a chance to jump to the other side until a remedy forms. The reality is you slowly allow quick remedies to become the norm. The line becomes blurred to the point that jumping becomes normal behavior. You hate to do it, but you love the results. There is a thin line between love and hate.

The support system of this world stamps it ok and you move on believing it's not your fault, that's just the way the cookie crumbles.

Discernment on the other hand redefines the word loser and embraces its new meaning. For example, change comes when something breaks. In the midst of that breakdown, the word loser appears, but in reality, preparation is laying the groundwork for a new path and greater actions.

In order for the invisible gifts to show itself in this temporal world you first must embrace preparation. If you embrace losing, guess what, you lose.

When your God breaks, you down embrace it, he is preparing and redefining you. How many times have you complain only to look back and say that action made the situation or me better.

Keep this in mind

From original sin that affected all kin to the remission of sins, I give praise to the father for the light of Christ within. It is clear to me that we are born to win.

Chapter 18

SIGNPOST AHEAD

Another reason for this book is to decipher the signposts on the roads of the playing field that carry warnings of up-coming obstacles. Faith is the catalyst needed in conjunction with words to work through these blocks of trouble. Discernment will strengthen your viewpoint.

We have already mentioned the fact that you were born to win from the very beginning. In this world when you make such claims out-loud it becomes a sign to the haters. You are recognized as cocky, arrogant, and foolish, and must be attacked.

The enemies of this world want to suppress your confidence in any way, shape, or form. They love it when they see you coming or you are rebuilding. They despise you and try to tear you down with their knowledge. I compare it to a system that makes the problem then recommends a remedy.

I really noticed it in my life shortly after entering the workforce. While at the campus of the University of Minnesota, I studied winners. Mentally I was under the tutelage of winners and world champions. People who looked at problems as a soda can to be crush on their way to victory.

They always spoke in future tense as if they already were on top and nothing could stop them. The positive aspect in their teachings was an uncanny ability to unravel the meaning of carefully placed signposts on the playing field. They taught signs are there for a specific reason.

The most important thing to understand about signposts is the road they sit on has been blazed already and they were left for our benefit. Having faith that this is the case is the key.

Not paying attention to signs in regards to disseminating their information becomes an introduction to multiple beginnings. Running pass any sign is unwise.

Information is taken in through one or more of our senses mainly by what we see and what we hear. Take seeing for example, most of us understand when you first meet someone it's their representative you are meeting not them, the reason we know that's true is after one becomes comfortable the real person emerges and your first impression will change.

You will have a better understanding of why you met their representative first. After all, when you meet someone for the first time do you let him or her in on everything about yourself? No. In fact, their representative has to make out a report, all the time looking for signs.

Discerning is easy once you know how. In the spiritual realm, we call this revelation knowledge. Revelation knowledge is rooted in grace. Grace is a blessing you have not earned. This is why you will continue to be blessed knowing you have a multitude of wrong doings.

Many use grace as a loophole. Believing they can practice an abomination and are forgiven every time. The signpost will read; I can't change God made me this way.

Under this scenario, the world would have you believe it is impossible to change some things about yourself or the situation. Does this make sense to you? Do you really think there are no repercussions, in the practice of doing wrong? That something is impossible for God.

If that last paragraph sounded like a contradiction then discernment, you must study.

The world says action is the process of moving physically in concert with your brain. The world's reasoning says one or more of your senses acknowledges information, which engages a thought that become a feeling that dictates movement. The mind becomes the root of action.

You see, you hear, you think, you develop a feeling and then you act.

Most signposts come in the form of people you meet. For example, you believe a racial or a disrespectful sentiment flew in your direction. Your mind says this person just insulted me without any remorse. I now feel like I have to respond in kind. Therefore, you say something equally insulting with no remorse.

You see, you hear, you think, you develop a feeling and then you act. The signpost read two wrongs make a right.

Your first movement was a response with words, now depending on who you're talking to it can escalates into more words, something physical, or one simply walks away.

Retaliating in kind places you in the twilight zone as explained in my last book "***Who you gonna blame it on.***" The twilight zone is a circle made up of pride, the blind leading the blind, irrational decisions, inflated sense of status, and distorted principles. These signs are not seen with the human eye.

Under retaliation, you have entered this zone through irrational decisions. Put on your gerbils uniform and get ready to run around in circles. Naturally, one must use one or more of the five senses to make a confident move, it's a scientific fact according to the law of science.

For the natural man or woman this is the natural way, but there is another way that can dictate movement. We will explore this way more and more as we move from recognizing the playing field to actions taken that move us in a spiritual direction.

Orville Gilmore Jr.

How do you know if you are a natural man or woman? These are the signs to consider.

If you make a decision based on what you see with your eyes, you could be a natural man or woman. If you have to touch it to believe it, you might be a natural man or woman. If answers are based on intellects, or levels of education you could be a natural man or woman. If you do not research, what you hear you might be a natural man or woman, finally, you live in the world of entitlement, and it's never your fault, you could be a natural man or woman.

On the other hand, a supernatural man or woman, after they have tested the spirits to see whether they are from God, can make decisions with no regard to those negative voices, which speaks to the spirit in you..In this respect, your ears will invoke the spirit and your mouth will speak with the guidance of that spirit.

In part, this is foundation building. These signs given proper consideration will change anything.

One of the biggest mistakes made is the belief that there is a democracy in the kingdom. The sign reads the best system is a democratic one. In a democracy, questioning everything becomes better through theories.

You end up actually thinking theories can change the system in your favor. Even worse is, believing you have a vote in the kingdom. Do you really think one can vote out what God has said?

Many places in the eastern part of the world have tried to copy the kingdom of God, where one *Man* fulfills all needs and runs on his commands. Some believe they have the power of God, which leads to many Gods. We in the West have called it communism, and have come up with our own system we call democracy.

As it turns out without revelation knowledge of self, and where one comes from you are trapped in your own understanding. This is the problem my friends.

The sign reads we believe in the theory of Big bang or Evolution.

The kingdom has one king that provides everything to everybody and has the answer for all things, impossible does not exist, time does not exist, and he is able. You must change the way you think to believe this. Do you really think the pot can tell the potter how to make the pot?

The road signs of today are reminders for the journey ahead. Take the yield, stop and wrong way signs for instance. When a problem becomes a threat, call it the yield sign. You need to slow your roll and take a picture. It's your wake-up call.

Next, obey the stop sign, this means shutting down your senses through meditation, fasting and waiting for directions. If you don't wait for directions, your speed will increase and you run through the wrong way sign.

The grace of your father as only he can have pleased exit signs at each point of need. Pay attention.

Use these every day signs as reminders and practice their meanings as described on this page. The Lord says he will instruct you, teach you the way you should go and watch over you even though you have the hardest of heads.

Chapter 19

VISIONARY

I am not saying do not think, I am saying change the way you think.

Take daydreaming for example. **Daydreaming is a mental action for the most part ignored, or misplaced in transition.** If you are caught daydreaming on the job or at school there can be dire consequences. Apparently making pictures in your mind is unproductive.

This action is really a closer look into the spirit of a person. One of the triggers to bring something out of the spiritual realm into physical manifestation is the action of daydreaming. It is a form of meditation.

Many have said, and proven that you must see it first in your mind before it is realized. In turn, this triggers a thought process that look for ways to bring that picture to life. How it works is one of the great mysteries of this world. The fact that it works should be all that matters.

If the daydreaming vision, give you ways to rob the poor and un-knowing for personal gain, you will also get those riches and the reward that comes with it. Discerning the roots of your daydreaming is huge. Does it come from the mind or the heart?

The vision should come from the heart. If it comes from the mind, double-check the source. Not knowing can land you in the twilight zone.

I can only say this about misusing the poor and un-knowing; you will not enjoy all of your gains, but it will look like you do. You will settle, mostly out of court. You are in the twilight zone, and this cycle will continue. You will always get the same result because you used the same formula.

Even in the natural world, they understand this is not the way. They say it is insane to do the same thing over, and over and expect a different result. When riches blind you, how can you see?

They say the mind is a terrible thing to waste. I say the mind is a terrible thing that leads you. Be led by the Holy Spirit.

If you are a daydreamer, it's time for a new understanding of how daydreaming and imagination will dramatically change your thinking process.

When your brain gives you an answer, we call it using intelligence. When the inner man or the Holy Spirit gives you an answer, this we call discernment. Choose one and be done with it.

Remember in the beginning discernment was the bridge of communication, after we fell down learning became the bridge of communication.

After the resurrection, discernment of everlasting life returned to us through the grace of God. It is now time to practice those ways taught to us by man's advocate, Jesus G to G.

Those visions are life-changing events. "Change the vision, change your life." One of my personal goals is to show people how pictures bring promises.

The key to turning your imagination into a reality is to act as if it is already accomplished. This is transformational and kingdom, like thinking.

All of us have had some kind of vision about our future. One must ask where did this vision come from, and how will I recognize the truth of it.

Vision is the original form of marketing. What you see is usually what you get. Notice what you are looking with, for example, if you are looking with the lust of money in the background. You develop an excessive craving for it, and decisions are based on it. The sight of it will dominate the greed for it. Lust is the operative word. You will have it along with the consequences of lust and greed, and once again, you enter into the twilight zone this time through the door of inflated sense of status.

Be very leery of the background. In most cases its money or power.

On the other hand looking at your vision through the prism of discernment, produces reflecting rays of light, that drive out the darkness, leaving an understanding of your vision. Using the gift of light is righteous. Use the light family, use the light.

It is important to remember darkness cannot drive out darkness only light can do that, just as hate cannot drive out hate, only love can do that.

Chapter 20

THE GREATER PROMISE

Most will tell you, the more you learn about a system, the easier it is to operate in it. Now this works both ways. Too much too fast too soon can be destructive. There was not always two systems in play. Will the pupil ever rule the master? I ask you what is the difference. It's up to you to determine which has the greater promise.

History has shown after the dust settles, there are only two sides to a story anything else equates to confusion. One side says naturally, there are many avenues, and guarantees of success in their system. The masters of it understand the information communicated from two or more of the five senses incorporated properly can manipulate any situation in your favor disguised as new information without saying a word.

This same information converted to an intelligible form of speech can manipulate the movement of flesh. Most consider you skillful, intelligent, and well educated if you understand these outlets. This is the realm of science.

Before you know it, the senses are running the show. The intellectual call this mastery, I call it the media.

Don't get me wrong the educational system has its merits but without the teaching of Jesus included the educational system is flawed, therefore the use of it is flawed, Furthermore, the use of science and theories for answers, promotes an ungodly system. This will result in the lifestyle of a gerbil.

The other side has one voice one avenue, and guarantees success based on promises. The only requirement is faith. The servants of this side understand one-man one way. This system works from commands, and communicates through the prism of discernment.

Orville Gilmore Jr.

No one on earth has mastered this system. The believers pray, and ask for understanding.

I have tried both. To make a long story short, I believe the redeemer holds the greater promise.

Whatever system you believe in work it, (***the natural or super-natural***) the belief in it will get results, although the results will be the opposite of each other. The question is which one has the greater promise, and how long will it last.

STOP! Don't think about the answer, ask your father for understand. It's the foundation for recovery.

We will go much deeper in more detail in my next book, about foundation building. Titled ***"The Foundation"***

Don't be mad when the hater prevails. He/she is just working their system to perfection. Why not work yours. If you find out at age 60 you are on the wrong tracks, it's not too late to get off. A train wreck is coming and you do not want to go out like that.

If you survive, who you gonna blame it on, who you gonna blame it on this time.

We said the vision of a spiritual man comes from the spirit within him. The inner man communicates with the spiritual realm. All of the answers that you will ever need will come from the inner man. Do you know him?

The natural man totally communicates through the five senses and believes the spiritual man's communication skills are irrational, and sometimes unrealistic.

Candidly, the natural man learns and the spiritual man discerns this major difference is worth studying. Discerning is simply outstanding judgment according to the study of the word. If you are not living in the truth, the inter-man will tell you and it hurts.

Learning is the scholarly process of acquiring knowledge from what is known as a formal education. Learning to discern develops an understanding of spiritual revelations. There is a big difference between learning and discerning.

Learning is nothing more than instructions broken down into hard lessons. Discerning is nothing more than hearing the word of God because he said his word repeated will not come back void.

Discerning over learning, both come with the same price, death. I am driving the points of discernment repeatedly because this is the master key to every door. It is the essence of success, which turns a blueprint into a promise.

Chapter 21

THE ADVOCATE

The main reason good people are so frustrated when they see evil prevailing is because they see a system working against them, and it seems like they're losing the battle. People must understand you need one to prove the other. Each has its own way. You work yours, and they work theirs. They both, serve a purpose, but with different results. The weed and the flower have grown together for as long as we can remember.

The advocates for evil will tell you *your time* comes after death, that you can work their system because you will be forgiven even after death. If you can live with that reasoning, good luck, prosper, and may the force be with you.

Their/our time is now

The key word is *time*. In their logic, they are locked in time and it's running out. Desperate times call for desperate measures. Therefore, if you work in their time arena you are also under time and your time is running out. Look around does this seem like desperate times.

How is it then that good people live well in desperate times? In addition, can evil survive? When your advocate arrives with you and your destiny in hand, will you be prepared to receive it?

Let me say this, darkness and time is a scary thing when it comes to knowledge of your maker. His assurances are already in place. Don't be scared, ask him what they are.

Let us prepare ourselves to receive the spiritual realm of understanding, and belief in the tools given spiritually to work the system of the great I Am.

Orville Gilmore Jr.

It all starts with words. Let there be light!

An ancient prophet said, the power of the tongue has life-and-death and if you don't bridle it, it will become corrupt. The advocate serves as your bridle when needed he is able.

It's not what goes in your mouth, it's what comes out that kills you. If you do not understand this saying, It would be wise to search out its meaning.

The words you use on a daily basis are worth exploring. This is another reason for journaling because you will find your own words from your mouth convicts or acquit who you really are.

Warning: listening and meditation will break you down, this will prepare you for your bridle, I call it a war wound, and I do have a story to tell.

Words on paper I compare to a mustard seed in regards to growth, where a few words produce a picture of a desired lifestyle. This is the substance of things hoped for and evidence of things not seen.

If words are the beginning and hearing comes second. Understanding what you hear will have a major effect on your decisions. Here is what I mean. Are you hearing with your ears or your spirit? *Stop*, and take a moment to think about it, seriously what do you come up with.

Earlier we talked about a reaction to a derogatory statement aimed at you, and your reaction to it. If you hear it with your ears as the natural man, the feeling brings a level of measured retaliation.

The enemy teaches, if you are slapped with such a statement don't turn the other cheek, slap back. This is a learned process. Their reasoning says you're just going to keep getting slapped, if no retaliation is your answer. They say no retaliation is foolish and may get you killed.

That's the job of the advocate.

If you hear those derogatory statements as a spiritual man there is a level of understanding of pain expressed, and compassion prevail in your reaction to it. The kind of words used in matters such as these will defuse the situation and peace will prevail.

If you believe in your advocate he will step in, a door of resolution will open, and you will slip away.

Discerning the situation says my advocate will control the situation, and if I have to fight, it's done for me. If you don't believe that and there's no way out for you but fighting by all means fight. A wise person will figure out what variables brought them to the brink of self-defense. You might have been able to avoid the whole thing.

It's not my place to judge but there are people who live their entire life without physical confrontation.

Here is one of my personal advocate stories.

At one time in my life, I was a bouncer at a bar in downtown Minneapolis, Minnesota. I was the second-biggest bouncer in that establishment. Friday and Saturday night, like many bars across the nation filled with party time people.

The place was set up like an arena with a huge circular bar in the middle, surrounded by a dance floor. From the ceiling hung a 10 x 10 chandelier that turned and placed a reflected star-like shadow on everyone and everything it touched. The place had two levels the second had bars in each corner and a lounge area in the middle. A railing would allow anyone to look at the people below, who were always dressed to the nines. On the first level, the back walls were lined with several exit doors and pub tables that stayed filled with people drinking and laughing.

What I found very interesting about this place was when you walk through the front door it was as if everyone looked at you and you could see everyone. Men looking for women, women looking for men, it was truly a Viking atmosphere. By midnight, the joint was packed and jump 'in.

Being a bouncer in places like this has its rewards and challenges. For me the sights and sounds of people having fun was a nice reward away from an irritating week of the other side of life. The job environment would constantly test the words of my philosophy.

Speaking of words the word bouncer, automatically to the macho-man, who had a little too much to drink, sometimes offered up an opportunity to test his manhood against bouncers, and dare them to throw him out on the streets.

On its face, throwing him out seemed like the only solution. On the other hand, turning the other cheek in front of a bar full of people seemed negligent. Believing the advocate will control the room, and fight for you, also seemed crazy. To those looking to see a fight walking away was not an option doing nothing might get you hurt.

You know the story, one night I was face to face with this very situation. I was summoned to a fight from a macho man who had a little too much to drink and trying to impress his friends.

It even got to the point some nights that bouncers from other bars wanted to fight the bouncers of our bar, to see what bar had the toughest bouncers.

It's Friday night and the macho man wanted to fight he stumbled through derogatory statements alone with a straight-up challenge, that he would knock me out and throw *Me* out the place.

The funny thing was everybody stood around to see what would happen. I had a choice I could fight him, I can walk or I could believe my advocate would not only speak but also control the room.

For a moment, the hair on the back of my neck stood straight out.

Without thinking, I said to him it's Friday night. I have authority here. One, you are drunk, if we get into a fight even if you win you will have considerable damage to deal with, do you really believe in your condition you can beat a sober man.

It's Friday night man, you are going to jail and you will be there for the entire weekend, and it's going to cost you money and maybe your job. Do you really want to do this? I then got into a fight stance.

His friends, the same ones that wanted to see him pounce on me grabbed him and said, man this is not worth it and they walked away.

I am almost 60 right now, and I have learned to handle every situation that way because I knew and have confidence in the advocate, to step in. More importantly I believe it's not my destiny to get into brawls.

That was just one situation. I believe, as you should that no matter the situation God is able.

Unconsciously I reached into the spiritual realm, (***help me Jesus***) and pulled down an answer that manifested itself in the physical realm and peace resulted.

You cannot tell me words don't have power. This is the way spiritual discernment works. A fight would have resulted if handled naturally. Discernment gave me many more nights of peace. I never got in a fight during that time.

Many believe that bouncer situation is okay but there will come a time when you must fight physically, and real peace will only lasts for a moment.

This is why many believe we will come to a violent end. Practicing this type of thinking will diminish any belief in the advocate.

The problem I have with this philosophy is it is rooted in the intelligence of man. Your belief will always equal your actions.

Revelation knowledge, which comes in the form of discernment, will allow you to live in peace, and fulfill your destiny. You will have to change the way you think to understand what ***I Am*** is saying.

Chapter 22

SPIRITUAL EXERCISE

Here is a spiritual exercise I use often when coming up with solutions. When you ask yourself a question, you will get an answer. It may not always sound right but it's an answer.

Answers predominantly come with framework and are possible.

What I do in my search is take the word time and impossible out of the equation.

Spiritually speaking, if God is the beginning, and the end where does time fit in. If your God is able, where does impossible fit in?

This is the kind of practice *I AM* talks about. I must warn you. Stepping out on faith is necessary, if you desire to live with the experience of knowing you are above time, and everything is possible. This type of practice will alter the way you think. These answers will lead to change, try it. Here's three examples.

1. How would your plans change if you knew you would be debt-free next Monday at 9 AM
2. What would you do knowing that dream job was yours before the application started
3. If you believed the bible held every conceivable answer what would you do

The answers in each case above, involves a new thinking process and preparation.

To the common person, this is foolish, and a waste of time. Logically, fear will dictate most responses. Whatever, your belief will give you confidence according to the level of faith you have in it.

The use of words for empowerment is one thing, believing them is another. If your words match your belief, dreams come true. This is another reason for starting a journal; it literally shows you what you believe.

Chapter 23

2015

There is clearly two ways of doing something or getting a result. The consequences of both have history, for all to see and experienced if repeated.

Once again, words are at the root of the answers. One of the natural system's greatest tools when it comes to learning how it works is that of association.

Today fear and the reaction to it dominate the masses across the world. The tools below work in association with each other to frighten you into a response chosen for that exact moment fear appears in you.

If you look closely, words set up the idea, the media shows you the corresponding pictures, the repetition of commercials will hammer it home and last, they will give you the solution at a cost.

If you turn, the volume of your senses down you will get a new understanding of how to handle fear, of all types. Below are four obstacles on the playing field that you can knock down with the greatest of ease using this new understanding.

- The idea
- the media
- repetition
- the solution

First, they want you to buy the idea that you can govern fear according to a level of safety. That's why you see so many commercials about insurance and security. Yet they both work in the dark.

Insurance companies dominate the airwaves, the prevailing idea is you and everything you own be covered, and whatever area in your life not covered with insurance will come back to haunt you and in some cases if you do not have it you are breaking the law.

We can't forget the small print that says don't worry about the cost, according to your income we have the perfect plan for you.

Beware boomers and those hitting the mainstream. This new team is picking up steam they've tighten up the seams for 2015

Security follows the same patterns you have to secure everything, the home, the car, your identity, even your route home. Alarm companies of all types are having a field day.

That's the outside now let's attack the inside

Then there is just for men, scantily dressed women and alcohol appealing to the lust of man advertised at every kind of relaxing event. Real men understand their responsibility on this earth everything else is just a toy It's no better for women but the idea is more subtle in their approach. I call it money'en-vanity.

For example, vanity is a target. Here you must change your appearance by any means necessary, the least of which is makeup, weight loss, or new clothing to claim authority in a man driven world. It is no accident scandalous revenge has a ring to it.

Then there is envy, this nasty little feeling is rooted in advantages that promote jealousy and achievement is its master. Oh! Let us not forget money.

Women will tell you whoever has the most money sits on the throne, but they believe who ever holds the money is the power behind the throne and he who sits is just a figurer-head. So Mr. Man, sit on the throne, I know better. Go figure LOL.

As a result, relationships fall under a brand new understanding, and that's not funny.

The concept of fear coupled with the media's interpretation and resolution of it will present a constant avenue of worry. To bring the point home and reinforce fear, repetition of it becomes instrumental for inducing division between men and women.

Beware baby boomers and those hitting the mainstream of things this new team is picking up steam they've tighten up the seams for 2015

Don't believe me; check out mayhem, he said even if you have insurance it will likely not cover extraordinary incidents.

Check for yourself how many times do you see the same commercial within the four hours you watch TV, the Internet with its cloaking devices and tracking systems will be repetitious in their inducement of any products you've looked at.

Now, that you are wobbly the right cross to the temple arrives

In the natural world, it's called the solution to a problem we created.

Now that we are all on the same page, *it is important to note at this point in this story, learning this way is nothing more than noise. My goal is to keep this noise at a level that your subconscious discerns it as waste and dismisses it as nothing more than hate mail.*

Their solutions naturally fit right in to the problem they helped create, and will always revolve around time.

Riddle me this; if you take time and impossible out the equation, alone with vocabulary, how will your mindset obtain an answer.

The greatest crime of time leaves you there to wait unprepared, and scared. It naturally says it's going to take time, in the meantime they rob you blind because you didn't have enough time and then have the nerve to tell you maybe next time.

Notice the use of the words time, it's confusing. The goal of a liar and deceiver is to put you in time. Your God has already delivered you.

For those looking for the short answer about time, I heard this revelation.

The enemy has no power in the spiritual realm he's locked out. His power lies in time and the belief of impossible. He got us to sin knowing the penalty was death, and judgment is coming. He believed death was the end of it, making it impossible to redeem man. He's left with time, not knowing when his is up. Therefore, he uses time as a weapon to keep you in time and hope you stay in darkness about how he was locked in time. He thinks his philosophy of impossible will defeat you.

The Scriptures say one day with God is like a thousand years and a thousand years is like one day. Where is time in this description? It also says nothing is impossible for God. What do you believe?

The average person buys a house believing that under the best scenario it's going to take double-digit years to pay for it. The thought of paying it off in one year not only did not cross their mind but impossible to conceive. Even if you play the lottery every day you believe you have one in a-billion chance to win and so you are prisoners of time, in most cases more than 30 years.

Intelligence tells you things will continue to go up in value therefore why pay it off when you can leverage it when the need arises for extra cash.

When financial systems take a hit, depending on your age, recovery may not be attainable. Here is their solution, file bankruptcy and start over, the media will always show you the millionaire filing bankruptcy several times and still has millionaire status. This is the natural and American way. It's one of the greatest magic tricks played by banks.

On its face, time, is needed to run a marathon, but a marathon runner will tell you he or she has run that race many times in their head before the actual event. When the marathon finally comes, they just run not worrying about time. The history of world records is my point. Have you noticed that in history all things are impossible until somebody does it? We have been to the moon, once thought impossible for example.

My point is your life will take a different direction if you believe you can pay off a $250,000 dollar house in one year, the word impossible being taken out of your mindset must be practiced, it will lift your belief system.

This type of thinking may seem strange but it will set the stage to pull your gifts out of the spiritual realm.

This road of discernment is made from the building blocks of faith. This road is spiritual in nature and already blazed by the son of Jah.

Taking these previous examples in consideration one should walk away with a better understanding of how words affect hearing, learning, and discerning. This combination goes to the root of all acts. This is one area I love to work on, and will work on for the rest of my life.

Chapter 24

MAKING SENSE OF MEDITATING

We mentioned earlier how spoken words affect everything from hearing to action. Even in silence, words hold promises. They are very few things the people of Earth can agree on meditation is one of them. Every culture on earth has used it in one form or another, for its effectiveness.

Every religion on earth uses meditation as a step along the path towards salvation. There is a universal understanding that meditation places you in a higher consciousness.

When I was transitioning out of the dark side I used extended periods of concentration thinking about the differences, sacrifices, and pain that I would have to deal with following that light which always seem far away. I would ponder how I got where I was.

The more I studied the word the more my life fell apart. At each major loss there would be crying, my teeth would grind together at the thought of some of the sins I committed, and sometimes I even bit my tongue.

I heard someone say, and I'm paraphrasing, Gods word goes out guarded and does not come back void, and words have the power of life and death. That was my stop sign. At this point, half of my work day spit daydreaming. I was single and lived alone. I was very thankful I have a job. I finally realized I could do nothing, I had nothing and needed help.

At this point, my mind stop racing and I relaxed. I started asking God and Jesus for help, I repeated some of his promises like, I would never leave you, anything you ask in my name I will give you and have faith. I asked him to show me what I was doing wrong, and I would correct it.

Little things that were good started tuning into big thing that was better than I could imagine. The formula was clear.

slow your roll, stop trying to do five things at once and relax. Looking back, those long periods of thought was meditation, which later made sense. The helper reminded me that my father in heaven has a plan, that I was part of a royal priesthood.

It was the greatest and hardest time of my life. I'll say this about the dark side you will be in shock an awe and amazed at what you can see in the dark. You will be convinced that it's good and good for you. I guarantee it.

But when the lights come on, the Emperor/Empress had no clothes. You'll either turn the lights off or leave. I exited that stage and left.

Warning: Every time you look back you add to the chances of going back. Word to the Misters, watch out Sisters.

Everybody has stressful and critical points in their life, it is at these moments a place is needed where electronics and people are not invited, better known as quiet time where noise is at an all time low. This is a *Yield* sign. Slow your roll, then stop and let to the traffic of life pass. *The Lord is trying to talk to you.*

The pace of the world is so fast at this time that most people run right through the yield sign

They typically say:

I've been assigned to the frontline, it's my time to shine, I put in my time. You can't be late if you want to be great, I've run through many signs in my time but have never tasted a fine. I hear what you say'in bro and I know what you mean but I got to get that green why you sweat'en me man I need a pension plan, so I run through a few yield signs

I'm just trying to get above the poverty line is that all you do is criticize what makes you better. I apologize. All I know is my hair is gray and I've been that way. I'm just trying to say you shouldn't play with traffic signs that way respect the right of way. Okay man, about that yield sign I'll stop next time.

The closer to silent you are the more the five senses shut down. The louder the word of God becomes. This is the source of meditation. The practice of this concept will convert words into faith. The practice of meditation allows you to understand the heart. Think about it. Meditation lowers the noise; it is imperative that you try this and listen. It will be the inner man communicating.

Then your ears will hear your father talking to you. If there is no love in the words it's not from God, but his enemy. The more you practice meditating the clearer the distinction. Confidence and strength will follow, along with disciplining the body. Your promises are in faith, a mustard seed worth is all you need. It is an important antidote and a gift.

How can you possibly improve unless there is some assessment of how you are doing? Without feedback, you do not know what changes will make you a better. Don't be fooled your life up to this point is the assessment. The practice of meditation yields the fruit of assessment. It will seem subtle, because you're fighting the fact, you have been horribly wrong. It's a hard pill to swallow, because you are addicted to yourself and can't possibly be wrong about everything yeah everything.

Each time you become quite meditation and discernment automatically turns on.

This is why the enemy wants to speed you up, he knows the noise coming from it will cloud your judgments. He has no access to the eternal realm, and cannot return to heaven. He now lives in the time realm and his time is running out. That's why he wants to keep you in time. Misery loves company. ***Glory-to- God, for revelation knowledge.***

Practice for the purpose of this book is nothing more than a self-regulating tool for building a foundation designed to understand the word of God. Meditation is the infrastructure of your blueprint.

If you think you do not practice, you have an inflated sense of status. The fact of the matter is you are practicing something, and if you can't define it you are in double trouble because you are line following the blind. Beware there are ditches out there.

Practice done incorrectly will actually be a barrier to your progress. The key is to slow it down to a point where your brain can operate faster than your mouth. Any time you cannot control your mouth mistakes will multiply.

Slowing the speed in which you operate will allow your practice to slow down. This will allow your vision to become clearer. This will allow your teacher to teach. Using specific words like *"it's possible"* and *"I believe God"* will allow you to understand your purpose and desire for truth. This allows your imagination to provide answers in a spiritual way.

You must always remember that imagination is rooted in improvement. For this purpose, meditation practice is very useful. Seeing it in your imagination is a road filled with the riches of fulfillment.

In the beginning, this will be frustrating but not fearful enough to sound the alarm of get out. Later you will notice, what once seemed hard became effortless. The world will mock this kind of practice. This is your sign that you are on the right path.

Whatever goals, skills, or dreams you desire the resourcefulness of meditation will provide consistent pictures entrenching the need for more.

Minions of hate boldly say, you people been praying for years and you are still in a hole. This is the product of frustration, which lives in the darkness of the words me my money and the power. All will reach for the hand of God, even the devil himself. Don't wait. You don't want to be taking your last breath to ask.

Chapter 25

LIGHTING STRIKES

Lightning strikes are those flashes of revelation that you must learn to capture.

Change comes in many forms, the most common comes after the fact and accompanied by pain. I suggest we become a little more proactive. Making strategic suggestions to yourself for one reading is another and of course hearing is the easiest.

All of these ways are methods of planting seeds in your conscious mind passed on to your subconscious to marinate in your unconscious mind, finally revealing itself as part of a blueprint. After said seeds are planted flashes of information I call lightning strikes start up.

Most of the time they are very brief but noticeable and they carry a wealth of revelation. The key is to capture these strikes. When you see them on paper the way you think will start to change. I carry a pocket recorder to capture those thoughts and later write them down in my journal.

Like many types of practice, repeated behaviors play a major role in your personal development. The difference is enormous in terms of the way we understand the use of light. It is a universal fact that the opposite of light is darkness. Darkness represents a lack of knowledge or enlightenment, also something undesirable. When one cannot see, darkness prevails.

The world equates black with death. What does the words prince of darkness mean to you? As you can see black is an undesirable word in any language. For example, the enemy says brown people are black, when plainly they are brown. Keeping with this fact, you can be fooled from the outside in, but not from the inside out, unless you strike out.

Orville Gilmore Jr.

Lighting strike journal

We all know when it comes to deceptive devices and devilish activity light is its greatest enemy. Sunlight is one thing inner light is another. The enemy hates them both, sunlight because it's most effective in darkness, the inner light because that light represents the spirit of God.

Consequently, light is our best friend. With any real friend, you draw closer to each other and develop a relationship with questions and answers. When the answer to a question comes unexpectedly days later, that is a lightning strike.

You do understand every day a little more privacy is taken away. It's really not funny but one of the first acts of man was too hide and then blame. It would be wise to act as if everything you do and say is recorded, because it's coming back someday, to either redeem you or crush you.

Do not be caught up in *"I don't have time"*, and rushed the action. Ask your God, Meditate, on the answer. If you knew, your father was the King; would you ask him for answers?

The world says he who hesitates is lost, okay that's not bad if you know what to do. If you don't know what to do immediate action seems to be the course. This means there is **no time** to think, you must have a predetermined answer.

Many have argued about the options one has if it comes to what to do if you are lost. The answer is easy, you simply ask for help from a friend. Asking a stranger doesn't seem to be the best avenue and is there such a thing as a safe strange?

Many believe that means a police officer, mail carrier or neighbor.

What if you are lost in terms of who you are, where you're from, and why are you here? My predetermined answer is ask God he is your best friend as a matter of fact he will light-up the trail home.

What I like you to notice in this question of lost, is how time is taken out the equation. Just asking is enough. Try this with small things, and like a seed it will grow, and multiply, eventually producing kingdom style thinking.

Let me say this in regards to tendencies and reactions. Your journal is your tracking device. It will show your history of reactions and tendencies of past situations. This will lead to questions that need answers. If you still feel there is no time left even after you ask, prepare for a train wreck, afterwards lick your wounds and try again. You are still learning grasshopper. Discerning comes before learning.

In the natural world, lightning starts on the ground develops on a higher plane and returns to the ground as a bolt of lightning not necessarily striking the highest structure. In terms of men and women on earth, you are the ground. The higher plane is the invisible realm of discernment, which returns to you as a lightning strike of Revelation knowledge from the holy spirit.

As a result shortcuts, are exposed for what they are, alternative routes. If you are still not sure, shuts down the noise of your senses with meditation so you can hear your father, he will give you understanding.

Right now, the world is trying to speed you up through the efforts of fear and time. Background noise is brought to you by your senses. They are under attack headed by the media. If you don't recognize this effort, fear will give you a new understanding of death by 1000 cuts. Finally, your knee will bend and you will ask. The good news is you are not alone everyone has to go through this process.

Let's walk through several examples of noise generated from the senses who work hand and hand with the rhetoric of the media. Afterwards, we are bombarded with their solutions. This then becomes plausible with repetition.

The amount of noise will determine your use of the word. The fact of the matter is lessening the noise makes you more productive. Distorted information can manifest itself into a lifestyle of ungodly oscillation.

All of the following senses fall under the direction of distractions if its usage is misunderstood they turn into multiple distractions.

The five senses are

1. Sight
2. Hearing
3. Smell
4. Taste
5. Touch

Take smell for example, it immediately accesses to your memory banks, this can lead to an emotional response, many times it leads to a purchase. Media marketers call it sensory branding. Before I understood its effects, I would buy now and worry about the payment later only to find later means robbing Peter to pay Paul this produces no gain. You live the life of a gerbil, constantly hitting the restart button.

In the gerbil years most of my solutions amounted to shortcuts, at the time I thought they were intelligent and logical, when I should have asked first. Every situation in this world is not new and explained in the reading of the word. I am sure you have heard the phrase, "there is nothing new under the sun. the word new tricked me.

Putting intelligence in front of understanding is out of order. What would you rather have first, understanding the word of God, or controlled intelligence?

I started out thinking intelligence would keep me in order. After capturing and recording several lightning strikes, a new understanding altered my performance. Understanding the way God sees it, brought my directional antenna in line with his.

Most corrections amount to slight adjustments. Understanding why there is order in decision-making was painful. This was a very small drop but the ripple effect was huge. If you ask your father to help you with discernment, he will, but if the noise is too loud, you will ignore him. Do you have ears to hear?

One of the loudest senses is lust, if not the loudest. It is rooted in sight and touch. When their volumes are high, the word is like a beacon, but the more we engage in the multiplicity of the information coming through the senses. You turn out the light to get busy. The only thing that matters now is satisfaction of the limbic system.

Another example is going to a strip club and fantasizing about having sex with the entertainer not giving a second thought about that person's welfare or name. What if you encounter a person who had so much to drink their judgment would be impaired, and its last call for alcohol? Who is really in control if a good hot piece popped up?

Don't get me wrong. There was a time in my life right before the club closed down; my boys and I would cruses like sharks looking for tipsy women to take home.

The brain rationalizes all of this by saying something like; even if they were supporting their little old grandmother, by giving them money, I'm helping too, this works for both of us. I'm pleasured, their pleased and/or paid. I thought it was a win-win, but I paid twice if you know what I mean.

The development of discernment will always shine light on revelation knowledge. Additionally, it's never absent of consideration for others and reminds us, usually with a vision of the reckless consequences stemming from actions without understanding.

Love and consideration for others and their well-being is paramount. One of the greatest revelations discernment brings is an understanding of grace.

Grace is not the permission to become a repeat offender, stop thinking that way, but consider the value of love for each other. After all someone loved you enough and allowed you to live under grace, knowing some of the devilish things you have done.

So how do we shut down this loudest of noisemakers?

First, one must understand our sinful nature is working against the Spirit of God living in us. God redeemed you by giving his son as payment for our sins. Know we must fight back. This is the short answer.

When you break down the short answer, it starts with quieting the noise. A voice will always remind you.

- You have been redeemed and restored to your original status
- ask me for help
- follow the shepherd
- prepare yourself to stand before your maker

There will always be the temptation to be led by your senses, what you do not want is to follow the lead of the tempter.

The door that opens the four descriptions above are found in reading the word as your daily bread, followed by meditation, which allows the lightning strikes of revelation knowledge to flow from God.

Meditation means turning your senses to quiet mode, and listen.

Lightning strikes come in a flash, gets your attention, makes an impression, and leaves with the speed of light. This is the main reason I carry a recorder it's one of the best ways to catch revelation.

Chapter 26

I'M JUST SAYING

There are 24 hours in a day, if you are locked in time, you do not have any for the word. You become a prisoner of the words impossible and time.

If you are a prisoner of the words impossible and time riddle me this. If one is the Omega and Alpha what is impossible, and where is time.

Life seems to be precarious, and full of perceptions and opinions. Most of the world believes money talks, and you never can have enough. The rains of life will come, and when they do, your money, better be right.

We are taught, the more ways you learn to use the system and practice those techniques that work for you, the less likely it is that you will be poor. The philosophy seems to be *"circumstance ethics"* where right and wrong is relative to the circumstances. Mastery of this philosophy will get you paid, in this world.

The leadership of this world has mastered the art of lying to look like and have the same value as truth. A magician would be envious of such a performance.

The kind of preparation this book is talking about involves developing spirit-to-spirit communication, mastering discernment, and practicing the techniques of faith.

The goal is to love long, prosper in peace and share what your discernment with others. One of the universal truths, states that practice makes perfect. Life is short, revelation will never stop coming you must be ready to catch.

- Are you prepared to stand on what you believe
- Do you practice what is taught by Jehovah
- if the one thing you desire came into your life would you be ready to receive it
- are you prepared to stand before your God

What you do with the types of practice in this book, will show itself, in the form of the decisions you make. The belief that you have received what you've asked will change your thinking.

Thank God, and light will shine. Don't believe me, ask your father.

Glory to God! There is no one like him.

Chapter 27

WHAT CAN YOU CONTROL?

For our purposes, control is a worldly restraint and self-regulation of your behavior.

Your present situation is nothing more than a starting point. Can you take a bad situation and use it to your liking? Yes, you can. There are only two answers to choose from when solving any problem. It's your way, or someone else's. Those of you who have tried one and switch to the other, have you made up your mind yet or are you still jumping grasshopper.

There is only one way. History has shown everything else adds up to confusion. The amount of light you let in is under your control.

Self-regulation is one of the main parts that make-up the infrastructure of worldly restraints, and adds value to the blueprint, that leads you to the promise of a prosperous lifestyle, which pleases your heavenly father. Adding control of self equals worldly restraint in my opinion

We must practice emulating our Lord and teacher. With no clear picture, map, faith or teacher you are left with your own understanding.

Restraint is the linchpin of change. Restraint will not stop the lifestyle you have now, its job is to limit your movement and keep you on a straight and narrow road. Most of the time, it shows up as a stop sign accompanied by pain.

The linchpin also serves as discernment, and keeps you from slipping off into darkness, if you stop and listen to yourself. You will hear spokes of the wheels, called your senses. Discernment will show you how to keep the noise of the senses at a low level. You then can hear revelation knowledge.

You have a choice you can do your best to use the words from the book given to the ancient prophets, or anything else. You have free will. Many wait until they are well into their life to make this decision. If you are one of them, it's never too late, if you believe your God is able.

Orville Gilmore Jr.

When my daughter was a preschool and still working on balancing herself, she would climb on a stool and raise her hands in victory. The first time she did it she barely made it, she was very happy about it.

She wanted to try again, I knew after multiple tries her muscles would tire, they were still developing and she would fall after multiple tries. I said let's do it again tomorrow. She kept insisting on doing it again. Finally, I gave in and let her try again. She did have more trouble this time, but she made it. I than said no more, you are going to fall you are getting weaker each time. She said one more time Daddy. I said no you are going to fall. I walked away two minutes later I heard a thumb; she had fallen off the stool. I comforted her and reminded her that I had said she was getting weaker.

After comforting her, she stopped crying, we had tea and cookies made on her easy bake oven. I told her she would get stronger. Afterwards she slept like a baby.

Months later when she was as big as the stool, after three successful times she stopped, and said; see daddy I didn't get tired. I never saw her try that stool again, but I did notice for the rest of her pre-teen years when I said no that was it.

Even though she had free will/choice, I could easily predict that she would fall down if she tried one more time.

I wanted her to understand. She was not ready for multiple tries, be patient, restrain your enthusiasm, your body will change, your muscles will develop a little more. Many things will become easy. She was quick to learn, but once she understood, she would get the job done efficiently.

Our father works the same way. He will tell you something, trust at a young age becomes faith as adults. This retains patients, which turns into discernment. If you can shut down the noise, you will hear this confirmation.

You can control the noise. You have free will use it wisely.

Chapter 28

UNFOLDING DOCTOR 'G'

This is the second of three books, with the third entering the marketplace in the fall/spring of 2016-17. This book has the means, and capabilities to recognize the action needed to engage spiritual discernment.

Standing alone, each book employs map-like features resulting in secure decision-making. This book combined with the first, (*"Who You Gonna Blame It On?"*) encompasses who you are, fittingly with the purpose of decisions, and the design of words. Making you more attractive to a lifestyle seeking you.

These fundamentals will get you started.

- Knowing yourself
- Define your decision-making properties
- Believing the design of the word
- Thanking your God

knowledge from this book help you recognize the routine need to visualize, then develop a blueprint that holds the promise of that vision.

The third book will cover balance, and the foundation you must stand on to withstand the winds of the one who hate and curse you. It's anchors are designed to strengthen your confidence thru faith, resulting in discerning the natural world systems, with the backing of your father. Who has the whole world in his hand.

Together the three books, *"Who You Gonna Blame It On?"*, *"Blueprint Promise"* and *"The Foundation"* represents self discovery, revising your plan, and how to store up your treasures in heaven where rust and thieves can't reach.

Orville Gilmore Jr.

I once had trouble understanding myself, and the way this world operates. I read many books on this quest in my *50* plus years, and finally, the word of God and this is what came out.

It's easy to change if you know how, thank you for reading and God bless you.

ABOUT THE AUTHOR

Orville Gilmore is a fifth dimensional thinker and educator. He is a talkative operative, with the conscience of at least five different characters, and a member of the royal priesthood, authoring parable books.

He is a 59 years old student of the narrow gate and road that lead to life. Orville spent his wonder years in Chicago, Illinois mainly under the tutelage of his mother and her four sisters.

He graduated from the University of Minnesota with a BS degree in work until you drop, and a Masters in discernment and consequences of the truth.

He has one brother, Dwayne and two sisters, Sherry and Loren.

In his free time, Orville enjoys watching sporting events on cable TV, especially championship play, going to movies and working out. He's retired and lives in America's playground.